The Mistakes You Make at Bridge

The big secret of success at this game of ours lies not so much in mastering complex bidding sequences and obscure play techniques as in avoiding the common and predictable mistakes that we all make from time to time. The player who discovers how to eliminate such commonplace errors can transport his game to an altogether higher level.

In this book two world-famous authors show how it can be done. In studying the well-chosen example hands the reader is sure to recognise the shortcomings if not of himself then at least of the other players in his circle. And recognition is half the battle. Knowing what to avoid, a player is less likely to err in the future.

The authors, well known to readers of the Master Bridge Series, have won equal distinction as players and writers on the game. For many years Roger Trézel was an automatic choice for the French international team, as was Terence Reese for the British. Both are European and World Champions.

'*The Mistakes You Make at Bridge* is a well-presented book that I can recommend to all players who have a general understanding of the game.'

– Jeremy Flint, *The Times*

The Mistakes You Make
at Bridge

by

Terence Reese & Roger Trézel

LONDON
VICTOR GOLLANCZ LTD
in association with Peter Crawley
1989

First published in Great Britain 1984
in association with Peter Crawley
by Victor Gollancz Ltd,
14 Henrietta Street, London WC2E 8QJ
Fifth impression 1989

British Library Cataloguing in Publication Data
Reese, Terence
    The mistakes you make at bridge.—
    (Master bridge series)
    1. Contract bridge
    I. Title   II. Trézel, Roger   III. Series
    795.41′5   GV1282.3

    ISBN 0-575-03424-6

Photoset in Great Britain by
Photobooks (Bristol) Ltd.
Printed in Great Britain by
St Edmundsbury Press Ltd, Bury St Edmunds, Suffolk

Contents

Foreword

It is not our intention in this book to present a complete museum of horrors. If we attempted to describe all the mistakes we have seen—including those we have committed ourselves—there would be no end to the story. We have concentrated instead on the sort of mistakes that quite experienced players commit all the time.

It is true that at the table even the worst mistakes often go unpunished. But not in this book. Bad bids and plays receive their due reward.

You might say that our aim was to put back on the road those vehicles that have settled in a ditch.

PART I

The Worst Mistakes

1

In bidding

IMMEDIATE BLACKWOOD

A Blackwood 4NT, asking about aces, should be used in response to an opening bid only with an exceptional hand. The fact that a side holds four aces hardly guarantees that twelve tricks can be made! This is a typical deal from rubber bridge:

```
              ♠ A K Q 3 2
              ♡ A 10 4
              ◇ 10 3 2
              ♣ J 3

♠ 5                              ♠ 9 4
♡ 9 8 3 2          N             ♡ K J 7 5
◇ K Q J 9      W       E         ◇ 7 6
♣ 7 5 4 2          S             ♣ Q 10 9 8 6

              ♠ J 10 8 7 6
              ♡ Q 6
              ◇ A 8 5 4
              ♣ A K
```

South, with his 14 points and five-card major, opens one spade. North strokes his chin, consults the ceiling, and leaps to 4NT. South bids a dutiful five hearts, showing two aces. Well satisfied, North goes to six spades.

West leads the king of diamonds and South is unable to escape the loss of two diamonds and a heart.

"That was jolly unlucky," says North. "Of course, you didn't have much for your opening bid. It was a rotten fit, both of us having a doubleton club."

"I think you did a bit too much," says South patiently. "You had quite a few losers. You might have bid two diamonds and followed with four spades. I think they call that a delayed game raise."

"Two diamonds on 10 x x! That'll be the day!"

There is another situation where 4NT, as a request for aces, is the wrong move. This is when partner has opened 1NT. A jump to 4NT is then natural, not Blackwood at all. In response to a 15–17 notrump it suggests a balanced 16–17 points, inviting a slam if the opener is better than minimum. So, what do you do if, over partner's 1NT, you want to be in a slam provided he holds a sufficient number of aces?

♠ A 3 2
♥ A 6
♦ K J 4 3
♣ A 9 3 2

♠ K J
♥ K Q J 10 9 8 7 5
♦ A 2
♣ 4

Over North's 1NT South must force with three hearts. Then, even if North's rebid is 3NT, 4NT by South will be conventional.

Some players use the Gerber convention, whereby four clubs, in response to 1NT, asks partner to show the number of aces he holds. The usual responses to this are four diamonds, one or four aces; four hearts, one ace; four spades, two aces; 4NT, three aces. Obviously you must not use this convention unless you have reached an agreement with your partner.

BIDDABLE SUITS

The normal minimum for an opening bid in a major suit is Q 10 x x, or perhaps A x x x in hearts rather than spades. It is permissible, however, if you play a strong notrump, to open a minor suit on a three-card holding such as K x x. Partner will not carry you to game in a minor unless he has exceptional trump support. Suppose you hold:

♠ 10 4 3 2   ♡ A 4 3   ◇ Q 3 2   ♣ A K 2

There are two reasons why you must not open one spade. One is that, after a competitive auction, you may end in a very hazardous spade contract. The other, perhaps more serious in the long run, is that your side may become the defenders and partner may lead a spade from a holding such as K x. If you are playing a 12–14 notrump you may hazard 1NT, but if you are playing a strong notrump you must begin with one club. Over a response of one diamond or one heart you can bid the weak spades on the second round, so you will not miss a good contract in this suit.

RESPONDING AT THE LEVEL OF ONE

Those writers on the game who talk always in terms of 'points' may tell you that you need six points to respond at the level of one and should pass when you hold less. This is quite wrong. When partner has opened a minor suit you need have no qualms about responding on the sort of hand that South holds in this example:

♠ A K J
♡ J 9 5 3
◇ 7
♣ A K 8 6 5

♠ 5 3
♡ A 10 7 6 4
◇ 6 4 2
♣ 7 4 3

[11]

North opens one club and East passes. It would be wrong to pass on the grounds that you held 'only four points' and still worse, in a different way, to respond 1NT, which would both exaggerate your strength (normally 7 to 10 for this response) and conceal your hearts. Bid simply one heart, intending to pass thereafter unless partner makes a forcing bid in a new suit. On the present occasion North would jump to four hearts, a very reasonable contract on the two hands.

Of course, it will happen sometimes that North will rebid, say, 2NT and be disappointed in your hand. Against that, by keeping the bidding open with one heart you make it far more difficult for the opponents to arrive at their best contract.

CHANGE OF SUIT AFTER A PASS

A sequence such as one spade by opener, two hearts by responder, is not forcing when the responder has passed originally. The South hand below might be regarded as borderline.

♠ 4
♡ K J 7 3 2
◇ A 8 6 4
♣ Q 3 2

♠ A K 6 5 3
♡ A 8 4
◇ J 3 2
♣ J 8

Pass by North, one spade by South, two hearts by North. Now South might say to himself, 'If my partner holds something like K J x x x x in hearts and K Q x in diamonds, four hearts will be easy, so I'd better give him a chance with three hearts.' Yes, but it's quite wrong to construct a particularly good fit when you don't know much about your partner's hand. Here, as you can see, four hearts would be a very poor contract, even though the North hand is fairly strong. And it is to be hoped you didn't think of rebidding two spades! That would be quite awful. Just pass two hearts and make sure of a plus score.

THE WEAKNESS RESPONSE TO 1NT

Over an opening 1NT, whether weak or strong, a simple response at the level of two (other than two clubs) is a weakness bid. The opener is expected to pass. Partner opens 1NT, 15–17, and you hold:

♠ 10 8 7 4 3 2   ♡ K 3 2   ◇ 4 3 2   ♣ 2

It is quite safe—at least, it should be safe—to respond two spades, which is likely to be a far more promising contract than 1NT. If your partner then bids three spades, reproach him; if he rebids 2NT, abandon him.

Except in one special situation it is quite wrong to take out 1NT into a four-card suit. Over a strong notrump you hold:

♠ A J 3 2   ♡ J 6 3   ◇ 7 4   ♣ 8 6 5 2

To bid two spades is diabolical. It is very unlikely that it will be easier to make eight tricks in spades than seven in notrumps, and if the opener has a doubleton in spades the contract will be ridiculous.

The only time when it may be right to show a four-card suit over 1NT is when an opponent has overcalled. Say that partner has opened a strong notrump, there is a butt-in of two hearts and you hold:

♠ A J 5 4   ♡ 4 2   ◇ Q 9 6 3   ♣ 7 4 2

It is reasonable now to compete with two spades. If the opener has something like K Q 10 of hearts and a doubleton spade, he may transfer to 2NT.

RESPONDING TO 2NT

When partner has opened 2NT you cannot make a weakness response at the three level. It is still wrong to bid a four-card suit, because partner will often raise with only three trumps. Suppose you hold:

♠ K Q 3 2   ♡ 7 5 3   ◇ 8 6 4   ♣ J 5 2

As probably you know, you can discover whether partner has four spades by using one of two conventions: Stayman, which asks the opener to name a four-card major suit, or Baron, which asks him to bid his four-card suits 'upwards' (three diamonds when he holds four diamonds, 3NT when his only four-card suit is clubs). However, it would be wrong to press for a suit contract on this very flat hand. Just raise to 3NT rather than aim to play in spades.

The situation is different when you hold something like

♠ K Q 3 2   ♡ 7 5 3   ◇ 6 4   ♣ J 8 5 2

Now you have a weak doubleton and it is reasonable to test the possibility of playing in four spades. But we are far from saying that you should always inquire for a four-card major when you hold 4–4–3–2 distribution. Suppose your hand were:

♠ Q 7 5 3   ♡ K 6 2   ◇ Q 3   ♣ 10 8 5 2

Now your spades are weak and you hold an honour in the suit of the doubleton. Just raise 2NT to 3NT rather than aim for a ten-trick contract.

BIDDING A TWO-SUITER

"You changed the suit! I thought you must be strong." This is one of the silliest remarks in the game. Suppose that the bidding begins:

South	North
1◇	1♠
1NT	2♡

North holds:

(a) ♠ K 7 6 4 2   ♡ Q 9 6 4 2   ◇ 4 3   ♣ 5
(b) ♠ A K 5 4 2   ♡ A 10 9 6 3   ◇ 5 2   ♣ 6

North's sequence is correct on (a), quite wrong on (b), which is worth a jump to three hearts, forcing for one round at least.

Generally speaking, it is right to use the Stayman convention only when you are looking for a 4–4 fit. There is not much point in using Stayman with a five-card suit, because then all you need is

[14]

three-card support. This is an example from rubber bridge of muddle-headed thinking:

　　♠ K 10 6 5
　　♡ A 4
　　♢ Q 7 2
　　♣ A Q 9 3

　　♠ 4
　　♡ Q J 8 5 3
　　♢ K 9 6 5 3
　　♣ 7 4

North opened a 15–17 notrump and South responded two clubs, explaining afterwards that he thought there might be a play for four hearts if his partner held four cards in the suit. Over two clubs North bid a dutiful two spades. South should have bid 2NT now, but instead he ventured three hearts. North bid 3NT and the partnership finally conceded 800 in five diamonds doubled.

It is true that, with an excellent fit, four hearts might just have been a good contract; but this was against the odds and South should have responded simply two hearts.

THE JUMP REBID OF 2NT

One of the commonest mistakes in the game is an unsound jump rebid of 2NT. It happens on this sort of deal:

　　♠ A K 6 4
　　♡ 8 5 3
　　♢ J 4 3
　　♣ 6 4 2

　　♠ 3 2
　　♡ A Q J 4
　　♢ K 6 5 2
　　♣ K Q 3

Not liking to open 1NT with a weak doubleton, South bids one heart. North responds one spade. Now South bids 2NT and North

[15]

raises to 3NT, which turns out to be a very poor contract indeed.

"You weren't worth 2NT", says North.

"What do you mean? I had much better than a minimum. I could have opened a strong notrump."

That may be so, but as a matter of convention a jump rebid shows 17–18 points. It says 'If you have anything better than a minimum 5 or 6 points we want to be in game'. On the present hand South should rebid simply 1NT. He has a little in hand, but what is wrong with that?

LIMIT BIDS

Playing with a strange partner, you can never be quite certain what he means when he responds 2NT to your opening bid of one, or raises, say, one spade to three spades. Is it forcing? Is it wrong to pass when you have a minimum opening?

This is a matter of system, and it is essential to have an understanding. Otherwise you may encounter a situation of this sort:

♠ A K Q 3
♡ K J 3
♢ 6 5 3
♣ 9 4 2

♠ 6 4 2
♡ Q 7 4
♢ A Q 4
♣ A Q 6 5

You open one spade on the North cards and your partner responds 2NT. You pass and he makes about ten tricks. After an incident like this it is wrong to blame your partner for under-bidding. Most American players would have given you the same response. It is sensible to settle in advance whether you propose to play 2NT as a limit bid. The same sort of situation arises when partner raises to three of a major.

♠ A K Q 3 2
♥ K 3 2
♦ 7 5
♣ 6 3 2

♠ J 10 8 7
♥ Q 6 4
♦ A K 6 5
♣ K 5

Suppose, this time, that you are South and that your partner has opened one spade. Unless you have an understanding that the jump to three is forcing, you must not bid just three spades and say afterwards, "I wanted to see if you could make a slam try: I didn't expect you to pass three spades." You are well worth four spades on your values. You are, in fact, strong enough to respond two diamonds and jump to four spades on the next round, which is a more encouraging sequence than the direct raise to game.

RESPONDING TO AN OPENING TWO-BID

Partner opens two hearts, the next player passes, and your hand is:

♠ 10 9 7 5 3 2   ♥ 5 4   ♦ 6 5 3   ♣ A 4

What do you say? Two spades? 2NT? No bid? It depends, of course, on how strong you expect the opening two-bid to be, but it is still a tricky situation. If the two-bid means 'about 20 points but not forcing', your best plan is to respond two spades and hope for a favourable development. If the opener's next bid is three hearts or three spades, you can go to game. Suppose, next, that you are playing the Acol system, in which two-bids are forcing for one round. Now you must make the weakness response of 2NT, because you have not enough for a positive response. On the next round you can raise three hearts to four hearts; if the rebid is three clubs or three diamonds you can mention your spades, and partner will know the sort of hand you hold.

THE RESPONSE TO AN OPENING 2NT

This type of hand often leads to a minor disaster:

♠ A Q 4
♡ A K 2
◇ A J 3
♣ K J 5 4

♠ 5 3 2
♡ 6 4 3
◇ K Q 10 8 5 2
♣ 3

North opens 2NT and South responds three diamonds on his six-card suit—what else? North, now, is 'interested', and there is at least a danger that the partnership will end in five diamonds, by no means a secure contract. Whose fault? Well, South's three diamonds was pointless. It is most unlikely that five diamonds will be a better contract than 3NT, and South should simply raise in notrumps.

This is another type of hand where players often end in the wrong spot:

♠ A 5 4
♡ K 6
◇ A K 4 2
♣ A Q 7 3

♠ K J 8 6 2
♡ J 10 3
◇ J 9
♣ 8 4 2

North opens 2NT and South responds three spades. As he has a ruffing value (short suit) in hearts, North raises to four spades. Neither four spades nor 3NT is cast-iron, but 3NT is certainly the better chance. Here South, with his relatively balanced 5–3–3–2 distribution, should raise 2NT to 3NT.

OVERCALLING IN THE OPENER'S SUIT

The control-showing overcall—or cue bid—in the opener's suit contains a special fascination for many players. Consider this sort of deal:

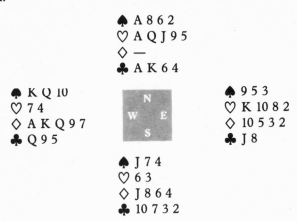

```
                    ♠ A 8 6 2
                    ♡ A Q J 9 5
                    ◇ —
                    ♣ A K 6 4
    ♠ K Q 10                          ♠ 9 5 3
    ♡ 7 4              N              ♡ K 10 8 2
    ◇ A K Q 9 7    W       E          ◇ 10 5 3 2
    ♣ Q 9 5            S              ♣ J 8
                    ♠ J 7 4
                    ♡ 6 3
                    ◇ J 8 6 4
                    ♣ 10 7 3 2
```

The bidding goes:

South	West	North	East
—	1◇	2◇ (1)	No
3♣ (2)	No	3♡	No
3NT	No	4♣	No
? (3)			

(1) Leaping into action—strong hand, control in diamonds.
(2) It is right to show the four-card suit, such as it is.
(3) "Sorry, I'm wanted on the phone . . ."

The mistake here lies in North's two diamond overcall. He has a take-out double—a strong one, but what is wrong with that? The bidding should go:

South	West	North	East
—	1◇	Dble	No
2♣	No	2♡	No
No	No		

Players holding the North hand are apt to say "I didn't want to double, in case you passed." Well, if South passes the double, because he has a diamond holding of the nature of Q J 10 8 x, North-South will obtain their best possible result.

South's cue bid, even though he doesn't hold ace or void in the enemy suit, is correct on this type of hand:

```
        ♠ 8 6 5 4
        ♡ 4
        ◇ J 9 8 5 2
        ♣ J 6 4

        ♠ A K Q 3 2
        ♡ A K Q 6 5 3
        ◇ 3
        ♣ 2
```

East opens one club and the bidding goes:

South	West	North	East
—	—	—	1♣
2♣	No	2◇	No
2♡	No	2♠	No
4♠	No	No	No

The cue-bid of two clubs is correct now for two reasons: (1) South is happy to force to game, and (2) he does not want to risk partner passing a take-out double.

There is a special way to express a very strong take-out double. West opens one club and North-South hold:

```
        ♠ A K Q 4
        ♡ A K J 6
        ◇ A 9 2
        ♣ 7 6

        ♠ 10 8 5 2
        ♡ 7 3
        ◇ Q 10 6 5 4
        ♣ 9 4
```

[20]

North doubles and South responds one diamond. Now North bids two clubs, saying "I have a big hand. Is there anything else you can show me?" On this occasion South is able to bid two spades and North will go to four spades. This contract is not cast-iron, but it stands a fair chance.

THE TAKE-OUT DOUBLE

The player on your right opens one diamond and you hold:

        ♠ A K J 5 3
        ♡ K Q 4
        ◇ A 8 5
        ♣ 7 2

It is quite in order to double, because if partner responds in your weak suit, clubs, you can transfer to two spades. On the whole, it is better to double than to overcall in spades, because partner might hold a fair suit of hearts.

The situation is different when your short suit is higher in rank than your main suit. See what happened to North on this deal from rubber bridge:

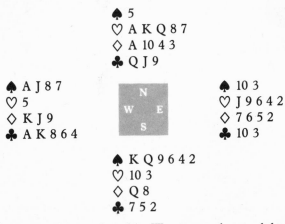

        ♠ 5
        ♡ A K Q 8 7
        ◇ A 10 4 3
        ♣ Q J 9

♠ A J 8 7   ♠ 10 3
♡ 5   ♡ J 9 6 4 2
◇ K J 9   ◇ 7 6 5 2
♣ A K 8 6 4   ♣ 10 3

        ♠ K Q 9 6 4 2
        ♡ 10 3
        ◇ Q 8
        ♣ 7 5 2

With both sides vulnerable West opened one club and the bidding continued:

South	West	North	East
—	1♣	Dble	No
2♠	No	3♡	No
3♠	Dble	3NT	Dble
4♠	Dble	No	No

There were several poor bids in this auction, but the worst was North's double of one club. A simple one heart is the best tactical move—no matter what some books will tell you about the limits for an overcall at the range of one.

The defence against four spades doubled went very smoothly. East ruffed the third round of clubs and returned a diamond, which ran to the jack and ace. Unwisely, in view of East's (imaginative) double of 3NT, South played off two top hearts, hoping to discard a diamond on the third round. West ruffed the second heart, cashed the king of diamonds, and played a fourth club, on which his partner contributed the ten of spades. After overruffing with the queen South had to lose three more trump tricks and finished five down, a little matter of 1400.

RESPONSES AND REBIDS AFTER A TAKE-OUT DOUBLE

One club is opened on your left, partner doubles, and after the next player has passed you have to find a bid on:

♠ A 10 4 2   ♡ 10 5 4 3   ◇ A K 6 5   ♣ 4

What do you say? Two spades? Two hearts? Neither is correct. You hold the values for an opening bid and your partner has shown similar values. You must make a stronger call, bidding the enemy suit, two clubs. This is not necessarily forcing to game, but it ensures at least one more chance. With this hand, if partner, over two clubs, bids a major, you can go straight to game.

Here is another problem, of a sort that often follows a take-out double. East opens one club and sitting South you hold:

♠ K J 8 4   ♡ A Q 7 6 3   ◊ 9 2   ♣ A 4

The bidding continues:

South	West	North	East
	—	—	1♣
Dble	No	1♠	No
?			

How many spades do you bid now? Two, three, or four? Many players would jump to three spades, but even that is wrong. Think of it in this way: if you opened one heart and partner responded one spade, you might raise to three spades, but only just. When partner responds to a take-out double you must allow for the possibility that he may be very weak indeed. On the present hand two spades is ample.

DOUBLING AN OVERCALL

Your partner, East, opens one heart, South overcalls with two diamonds, and you hold:

(1)	♠ A 4	(2)	♠ J 5
	♡ J 9 6 3		♡ 7 4
	◊ A J 8 5		◊ K 10 8 6 4 2
	♣ J 4 2		♣ 9 5 3

Do you double on (1)? Wrong, because you have good support for your partner's suit. In general, do not make a penalty double until you have expressed support. Here you should raise to three hearts.

On (2) you may be confident of defeating two diamonds, but it is still wrong to double on trump strength alone. Suppose North takes out the double of two diamonds into two spades, and your partner doubles that. Now you are very poorly placed; you are not happy to defend against two spades doubled, but what can you do?

[23]

Again your partner opens one heart, South overcalls with two diamonds, and you hold:

(3)   ♠ Q 8 5   (4)   ♠ K 7 4 2
       ♡ K 4   ♡ 3
       ◇ Q 10 7 2   ◇ A 5 4
       ♣ K 7 4 3   ♣ Q 10 6 4 3

You have an obvious double on (3). It is also right to double on (4), partly because there is no other good way to express your values, partly because this double may turn out to be very successful, and partly because it won't be a tragedy if they make two diamonds doubled. (It would be dangerous, with a similar holding, to double a major suit at the two level.)

It is not necessarily wrong to double an overcall when you hold a suit of your own, as in the following example:

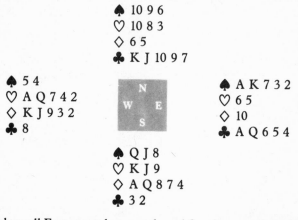

                 ♠ 10 9 6
                 ♡ 10 8 3
                 ◇ 6 5
                 ♣ K J 10 9 7

♠ 5 4   ♠ A K 7 3 2
♡ A Q 7 4 2   ♡ 6 5
◇ K J 9 3 2   ◇ 10
♣ 8   ♣ A Q 6 5 4

                 ♠ Q J 8
                 ♡ K J 9
                 ◇ A Q 8 7 4
                 ♣ 3 2

At love all East opened one spade and South overcalled with two diamonds. This is the worst type of overcall: South has a defensive type of hand, and two diamonds will lead nowhere. One of the present authors, sitting West, doubled two diamonds, and all passed.

It proved a cruel affair for South. After a spade to the king and a heart back, the defence took the first eight tricks, arriving at this position with East on lead:

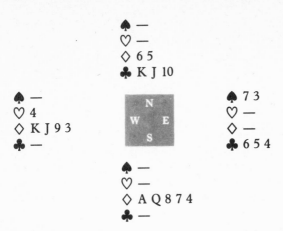

```
                    ♠ —
                    ♡ —
                    ◇ 6 5
                    ♣ K J 10
♠ —                                    ♠ 7 3
♡ 4                   N                 ♡ —
◇ K J 9 3          W     E              ◇ —
♣ —                   S                 ♣ 6 5 4
                    ♠ —
                    ♡ —
                    ◇ A Q 8 7 4
                    ♣ —
```

When East led a club South ruffed with the seven and was overruffed by the nine. West exited with a heart. Now South ruffed with dummy's six of diamonds and underruffed with the 4; thus he was able to end-play West.

"That was an underruffing coup; very pretty", said West, as he entered 900 above the line. (True, South could have obtained the same result by ruffing with the eight and exiting with a low trump.)

WHEN TO TAKE OUT A PENALTY DOUBLE

In what circumstances do you take out partner's double of an overcall? For example, at equal vulnerability you open one spade, second hand overcalls with two diamonds, and your partner doubles. After a pass by fourth hand you hold:

    ♠ K J 9 7 4   ♡ A 8 3   ◇ 6 2   ♣ K Q 6

Some players would take out the double on the grounds that they held a minimum opening. That is absolutely wrong.

There are two occasions when it will usually be right to remove a double after this kind of sequence. Suppose you hold:

    ♠ K J 9 7 4   ♡ A 10 8 5   ◇ —   ♣ K J 4 2

It is wrong to pass and say afterwards "As I was void of diamonds I thought you must hold a long string of them." First, if the diamonds are, say, 6–4–3–0 round the table, your partner's diamond holding may be cut up and produce fewer tricks than he expected. Second, since partner doubled two diamonds after you had opened one spade, he is doubtless short of spades and may hold four or five hearts. You should certainly remove the double into two hearts—not two spades. The defence on this type of hand tends not to go well even if partner does hold a long string, five or six. He will be trump-bound, as it is called, forced to ruff and make disadvantageous leads from his own hand.

In general, too, you should remove a low-level double when you hold a marked two-suiter. The bidding begins:

South	West	North	East
1♡	2♣	Dble	No
?			

South holds:

♠ K 4   ♡ A 10 8 6 3   ◇ K Q 10 9 5   ♣ 3

He should take out the double into two diamonds, because if partner has some length in diamonds the defence against two clubs may go poorly.

THE LEAD WHEN 3NT IS DOUBLED

When a partner who has bid a suit doubles 3NT, he is asking you to lead his suit.

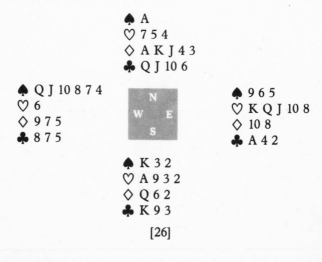

[26]

The bidding goes:

South	West	North	East
—	—	1◇	1♡
2NT	No	3NT	Dble
No	No	No	

After the double of 3NT West, who might otherwise have tried the queen of spades, must lead his partner's suit. This surely holds the declarer to eight tricks.

When a partner who has not entered the bidding doubles the final contract in notrumps, this means that he has a powerful holding in the first suit bid by the dummy. It will usually be correct to lead this suit.

Finally, what do you suppose is the message of a double after this sequence:

South	West	North	East
1♣	1♠	2♡	No
2NT	No	3NT	Dble
No	No	No	

Is East requesting a spade, West's suit, or a heart, bid by dummy? In principle, the double asks the overcaller to lead his own suit. This may be the full hand:

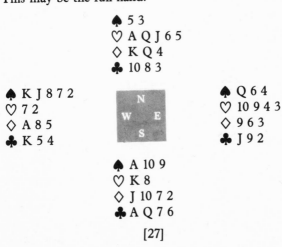

```
                ♠ 5 3
                ♡ A Q J 6 5
                ◇ K Q 4
                ♣ 10 8 3
♠ K J 8 7 2                    ♠ Q 6 4
♡ 7 2             N            ♡ 10 9 4 3
◇ A 8 5       W     E          ◇ 9 6 3
♣ K 5 4          S            ♣ J 9 2
                ♠ A 10 9
                ♡ K 8
                ◇ J 10 7 2
                ♣ A Q 7 6
```

West must lead a spade to defeat the contract. East's double is dangerous in a way, but he must realize that it may be difficult otherwise for his partner to lead a spade.

DOUBLING A SLAM CONTRACT

One of the most expensive errors in the game is to double a slam contract because you hold two likely-looking tricks, such as two aces. If opponents have contracted for a slam, the odds are that they *know* they are missing two aces and that there is a void in one of the suits. A double of this kind stands to gain 50 or a 100 and to lose six times as much if there is a redouble and the contract is made.

An unexpected double of a slam contract, when there has been little or no competitive bidding, is a "Lightner double". The message is "Don't make the obvious lead: in particular, don't lead any suit that our side has bid." Sometimes the Lightner double asks for a lead of a suit bid by the eventual dummy; sometimes the doubler has a void and will be able to ruff at trick one.

For example, East, who has overcalled in spades, doubles an eventual six diamonds and West has to lead from:

♠ 6 3   ♡ J 8 7 5 4 2   ◇ 9 4   ♣ Q 6 3

East certainly does not want a spade lead. In all probability he is void of hearts and will be able to ruff.

THE SOS REDOUBLE

Most players have heard of SOS redoubles, but their partners, at any rate, may fail to distinguish between the two types of redouble. Compare these two sequences:

	South	*West*	*North*	*East*
(1)	1♣	Dble	No	No
	Redble			
(2)	1♣	No	No	Dble
	Redble			

In the first example South, if he held a fair suit of clubs, could pass the double. His redouble means "I have short clubs; will you show your best suit?"

In the second example South is not so far in the situation of being about to play in one club doubled. The redouble, when he has been doubled on his right, indicates that he has a maximum opening bid of one. It encourages partner to double any bid by West.

Neither of these sequences is very likely to occur at the table, but they illustrate the principle. Another form of rescue redouble occurs when partner's overcall has been doubled, in a sequence of this kind:

South	West	North	East
1♣	1♠	Dble	Redble

If East were happy to play in one spade doubled, he would pass. The redouble is SOS, suggesting a hand of this kind:

♠ —   ♡ J 9 7 4 3   ◇ 10 8 7 2   ♣ J 6 4 3

The redouble says to partner, "Try something else—even clubs if you have some length in that suit." Quite often the best resting-place is the minor suit that has been bid by the opponents.

2

In defence

UNDERLEADING AN ACE

In a notrump contract it is perfectly in order to underlead an ace from a long suit such as A Q x x x. To underlead an ace against a suit contract is dangerous. Occasionally it will win a surprise trick, but it will cost a trick far more often.

```
              ♠ K 3 2
              ♡ J 2
              ◇ K Q J 3
              ♣ K 6 4 2

  ♠ A 10 8 6 5              ♠ J 9 7
  ♡ 3              N        ♡ K Q 10
  ◇ 8 6 5      W     E      ◇ 10 9 7 4
  ♣ A 10 8 3       S        ♣ J 9 7

              ♠ Q 4
              ♡ A 9 8 7 6 5 4
              ◇ A 2
              ♣ Q 5
```

This is a deal from tournament play, where the same hand was played at several tables. As you can see, East-West can take four tricks against the normal contract of four hearts. Yet the contract was made at more than half the tables!

A normal sequence would go something like this:

South	West	North	East
—	—	1◇	No
1♡	No	1NT	No
4♡	No	No	No

Sitting West, what would you lead? There is not much to recommend a diamond, the suit bid by North. It is seldom right to lead a singleton trump, as this may kill partner's Q x x or K J x. Several players underled one of the black aces. They were leading through the player who had opened the bidding, and this *might* have been clever. As the cards lay, it was fatal, because after winning the first trick the natural play for the declarer was to cash the ace of hearts and then play three rounds of diamonds, discarding the loser in the suit that had been led. Note that a diamond lead is no better, because then South will cash the ace of hearts, as before, and follow with three more diamonds, discarding either two spades or two clubs.

Suppose, next, that you lead ace of spades and see the dummy. Is it reasonable, now, to try a low club? Partner might hold the queen of clubs and only one trick in the trump suit.

This defence is understandable, but there is an argument against it. South should ask himself, Why did West begin with this lead of an ace in front of the opening bidder? The answer, surely, is that West held both black aces. A sensible declarer will not go wrong.

ENCOURAGING SIGNALS

When a player is pleased with his partner's lead he must not hesitate to play the highest card he can afford.

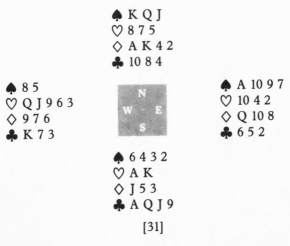

```
              ♠ K Q J
              ♡ 8 7 5
              ◇ A K 4 2
              ♣ 10 8 4
♠ 8 5                          ♠ A 10 9 7
♡ Q J 9 6 3      N            ♡ 10 4 2
◇ 9 7 6       W     E         ◇ Q 10 8
♣ K 7 3          S            ♣ 6 5 2
              ♠ 6 4 3 2
              ♡ A K
              ◇ J 5 3
              ♣ A Q J 9
```

[31]

South plays in 3NT and West leads the queen of hearts. Suppose that East, content with the lead, drops the four. South will win with the king, cross to dummy with a diamond, and run the ten of clubs. This is a shrewd move, because West may not be certain of the heart position. Indeed, West may well place South with A K 10 or A K 10 x of hearts. If West leads a spade or a diamond at this point, South will easily make the contract.

Since it is normal to lead a low card from Q J x x or Q J x x x, East should place his partner with Q J 9 and confidently encourage with the ten on the first trick. Then the defence can hardly go wrong.

This is another situation where a defender must not fail to emit a clear signal:

```
                  ♠ A 5 2
                  ♡ J 6 3
                  ◇ A K J 2
                  ♣ 8 7 3

  ♠ K Q 7                          ♠ J 9 4 3
  ♡ 9 5 2          N               ♡ 7
  ◇ 10 9 4       W   E             ◇ Q 8 6
  ♣ J 5 4 2        S               ♣ A Q 10 9 6

                  ♠ 10 8 6
                  ♡ A K Q 10 8 4
                  ◇ 7 5 3
                  ♣ K
```

The bidding goes:

South	North
1♡	2◇
2♡	4♡
No	

West leads the king of spades and East, let us say, contributes a grudging four. South will surely play low, partly because the spades may be divided 5–2 and partly because there is a chance that West will not continue the suit. And indeed West may well fear that declarer is playing a Bath coup, holding up with J x x and hoping for a spade continuation. If West switches to a diamond, South will draw trumps and establish a long diamond for a spade discard.

When West leads the king of spades it must be clear to East that his partner holds K Q x or possibly K Q 10 x. In any case, East can easily afford to signal clearly with the nine. So long as West continues with a second spade at trick two, South is likely to lose two spades, a diamond and a club.

WHEN NOT TO SIGNAL

Question: What is worse than a partner who never signals in defence? Answer: A partner who signals all the time. Sorry, but bridge is a difficult game!

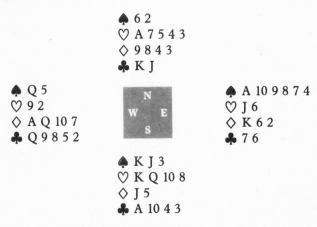

```
                    ♠ 6 2
                    ♡ A 7 5 4 3
                    ◇ 9 8 4 3
                    ♣ K J
  ♠ Q 5                              ♠ A 10 9 8 7 4
  ♡ 9 2                              ♡ J 6
  ◇ A Q 10 7                         ◇ K 6 2
  ♣ Q 9 8 5 2                        ♣ 7 6
                    ♠ K J 3
                    ♡ K Q 10 8
                    ◇ J 5
                    ♣ A 10 4 3
```

South plays in four hearts and West leads a low trump. After drawing a second round South plays three rounds of clubs, ruffing in dummy. On this trick East signals with the ten of spades. Now the declarer, unless he regards East as a particularly subtle player, will guess correctly and make his contract. East should discard a low spade on the third round of clubs and play low again when a spade is led from dummy.

The spade signal was particularly foolish here because the defence would surely need one or two spade tricks to defeat the contract. Sooner or later, a round of spades would be played, and East should not aim to give the declarer any assistance.

HONOUR SURRENDERED

There are many situations where it is poor play to split honours in front of the declarer. This position is elementary:

A 3 2

5   J 10 6 4

K Q 9 8 7

When declarer leads the ace from dummy and follows with the three, East must not, of course, contribute the jack or ten. Similarly:

7 5 3

8   Q J 6

A K 10 9 4 2

When the three is led from dummy, East must not contribute the jack. South may be intending to play for the drop, but the sight of the jack may persuade him to win with the king, return to dummy, and finesse on the next round.

To play the jack in the last example would be a disaster if partner held the singleton king or ace and might be a disaster if West held a singleton ten.

There are many situations where the general principle of covering an honour with an honour may lead a defender into a foolish play.

J 7 4

Q   K 6 3

A 10 9 8 5 2

Obviously it will be disastrous here for East to cover dummy's jack with the king. This is another example of the same kind:

Q 8 5 2

A   K 4

J 10 9 7 6 3

South leads the queen from dummy, tempting East to contribute the king.

The general purpose of covering an honour with an honour is to promote a lower honour. It should be obvious to East in the last two examples that covering with the king, when South is marked with length, is much more likely to cost a trick than to gain one.

FINESSING AGAINST PARTNER

To finesse against partner is in many cases a criminal error. For example:

9 6 4

A 10 5 3   K J 7

Q 8 2

Defending against 3NT, West leads a low card. Not many players would make the mistake of finessing the jack—at least they wouldn't do it twice with the same partner!

Oddly enough, this type of play may be correct against a suit contract when you can be fairly sure that partner has not underled an ace. Suppose this is the distribution:

9 4 2

Q 10 8 5 3   K J 7

A 6

West leads the five of a side suit. If East plays the king and declarer the ace, East cannot be sure who holds the queen and whether there is another possible trick for the defence. It is good play here to insert the jack on the first trick. When this forces the ace, East knows more about the hand.

[35]

There are many situations where it is correct to finesse against the dummy.

Q 4 3

J 9 6 5 2   K 10 7

A 8

West leads low against 3NT and a low card is played from dummy. Now it is correct for East to play the ten. He is not finessing against his partner, but against the dummy. As you can see, the finesse of the ten holds declarer to one trick in the suit.

This is another common situation:

A 10 3

Q 9 7 2   J 8 5

K 6 4

When West leads low and the three is played from dummy, East must play the eight, finessing against dummy's ten. If the king and queen were exchanged, the play of the eight would save a trick in the same way.

East is put to the test when the cards lie like this:

A 9 6

K 8 5 2   J 7 4 3

Q 10

Defending against a notrump contract, West leads the two and dummy plays low. Note that East can save a trick for his side by inserting the seven. This would be a losing play only if his partner had led low from K Q x x or Q 10 x x.

WHICH CARD TO RETURN

West leads low against a contract in notrumps, East plays an honour and holds the trick. If East holds three cards, such as A 9 5, he will normally return the nine; but which card should he play from A 9 5 2 or A 9 5 4 2? These are tricky problems to which there is no simple answer.

8

Q 9 7 6   A 10 5 3

K J 4 2

West leads the six and East wins with the ace. While it is normal to return the fourth best, in this case the ten is a better choice. If East returns the three, South will play low, and it will take some time before the defenders can establish three winners. In this case partner's lead of a relatively high card, the six, is an indication that he holds strong intermediates.

When the defender who wins the first trick holds five cards, it is correct to return the original fourth best. Say that this suit is led against 3NT:

5

Q 10 7 4   A 8 6 3 2

K J 9

West leads the four, East wins with the ace and returns the three. Quite often, West will capture the jack with the queen and fail to return the suit. "I placed the declarer with K J 9 8", he will say afterwards.

Note that this is a very poor excuse. If South holds K J 9 8, what is East's holding? Would he have led back the three from A 6 3 2? Obviously not, and it is, of course, unlikely that South will have as strong a holding as K J 9 8 6, since he has not mentioned the suit. After winning with the queen West must return the ten, making sure that the later run of the suit is not blocked.

There are, of course, many times when a defender should not return his partner's lead. Here is an example where the correct card may not be obvious:

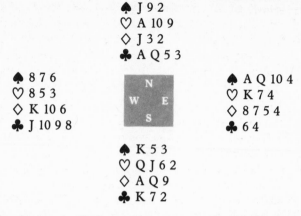

```
              ♠ J 9 2
              ♡ A 10 9
              ◇ J 3 2
              ♣ A Q 5 3
♠ 8 7 6                        ♠ A Q 10 4
♡ 8 5 3          N             ♡ K 7 4
◇ K 10 6      W     E          ◇ 8 7 5 4
♣ J 10 9 8       S             ♣ 6 4
              ♠ K 5 3
              ♡ Q J 6 2
              ◇ A Q 9
              ♣ K 7 2
```

South plays in 3NT and West leads the jack of clubs. It would normally be good play to win this trick in dummy, leaving East uncertain whether his partner had led from J 10 or K J 10, but on this occasion South wants to be in his own hand to test the hearts. He runs the queen and East captures the second round. What should East play now?

There is not much point in returning partner's club lead, and not much can be expected from the diamonds. The card to play is the queen of spades. South wins with the king and can make eight tricks, but as soon as he loses the lead to West he will lose three more tricks and finish one down.

The defence on the following hand is more difficult:

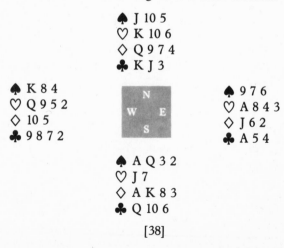

```
              ♠ J 10 5
              ♡ K 10 6
              ◇ Q 9 7 4
              ♣ K J 3
♠ K 8 4                        ♠ 9 7 6
♡ Q 9 5 2        N             ♡ A 8 4 3
◇ 10 5        W     E          ◇ J 6 2
♣ 9 8 7 2        S             ♣ A 5 4
              ♠ A Q 3 2
              ♡ J 7
              ◇ A K 8 3
              ♣ Q 10 6
```

[38]

West leads the nine of clubs against 3NT and South plays low from dummy. If he is allowed to win this trick he will make the contract easily. East can see that there is no future in clubs, so he takes the ace and looks for some way of establishing five tricks. There is really no chance to do damage in spades or diamonds; the only hope is to establish tricks in hearts. Observe the effect of a low heart at trick two: West plays the nine, forcing dummy's ten, and when West comes in later with the king of spades he will advance the queen of hearts, establishing five tricks for the defence.

COVERING AN HONOUR WITH AN HONOUR

The old warning to cover an honour with an honour may have been excellent advice in the days of whist, but it is a rule, if you call it a rule, to which there are many exceptions. To begin with, it is almost always wrong to cover the first of two honours in sequence.

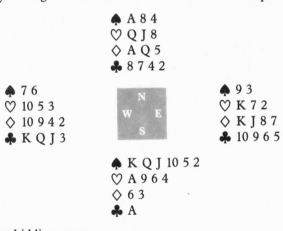

```
                    ♠ A 8 4
                    ♡ Q J 8
                    ◇ A Q 5
                    ♣ 8 7 4 2
 ♠ 7 6                                    ♠ 9 3
 ♡ 10 5 3              N                  ♡ K 7 2
 ◇ 10 9 4 2        W       E              ◇ K J 8 7
 ♣ K Q J 3             S                  ♣ 10 9 6 5
                    ♠ K Q J 10 5 2
                    ♡ A 9 6 4
                    ◇ 6 3
                    ♣ A
```

The bidding goes:

South	North
1♠	2◇
3♠	4NT
5♡	6♠
No	

[39]

West leads the king of clubs and since the diamond finesse is wrong South cannot afford to lose any trick in hearts. Suppose that at an early stage he leads the queen of hearts from dummy. East must not cover the first of touching honours. If he does, then South will win with the ace and finesse the eight on the next round.

The play is quite simple for East, who can see dummy's Q J 8 of hearts. Suppose, instead that the hearts were distributed in this fashion:

A 8 4

K 7 2   10 5 3

Q J 9 6

When South leads the queen, how does West know that it would be wrong to cover? He cannot be absolutely sure, but think of it in this way; if South held Q x x, would he lead the queen from hand? If not a complete beginner, he would lead from dummy towards the queen.

Some puzzling situations arise when the defender holds K x. Dummy leads the queen in this position:

Q J 9 3

10 8 7   K 4

A 6 5 2

Say that this is the trump suit and that South leads the queen from dummy. East's best chance is to play low. South may then follow with the jack from dummy, attempting to pin 10 x in the West hand.

It is generally correct, on the other hand, to cover when you can see *two* honours on your left.

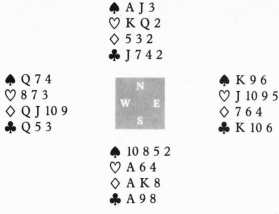

```
              ♠ A J 3
              ♡ K Q 2
              ◇ 5 3 2
              ♣ J 7 4 2

♠ Q 7 4                        ♠ K 9 6
♡ 8 7 3          N            ♡ J 10 9 5
◇ Q J 10 9    W     E         ◇ 7 6 4
♣ Q 5 3          S            ♣ K 10 6

              ♠ 10 8 5 2
              ♡ A 6 4
              ◇ A K 8
              ♣ A 9 8
```

South plays in 3NT and West leads the queen of diamonds. South wins the second round and the correct play now is a low spade to the jack. He can make three tricks in spades if West holds K Q or a doubleton king or queen. As the cards lie, this play fails. However, South might begin by leading the ten from hand. Now, as you see, it is vital for West to cover.

True, the spade distribution might have been:

A J 3

Q 7 4   8 6 2

K 10 9 5

Now it would be a mistake for West to cover the ten with the queen. There is no complete solution to problems of this kind. It is probably wrong to cover, because in general you wouldn't expect declarer to lead the ten unless he held the nine also.

This deal presents an unusual situation:

```
                    ♠ 3 2
                    ♡ 6 4
                    ♢ 8 3
                    ♣ A Q 9 6 4 3 2
    ♠ J 10 9 8                        ♠ Q 7 6 4
    ♡ 9 2          ┌─────────┐        ♡ Q J 10 7 3
    ♢ K 10 5       │ N       │        ♢ Q 9 7 4
    ♣ K 10 8 7     │ W     E │        ♣ —
                   │     S   │
                   └─────────┘
                    ♠ A K 5
                    ♡ A K 8 5
                    ♢ A J 6 2
                    ♣ J 5
```

North opens three clubs and South transfers to 3NT. West leads the jack of spades. South wins and advances the jack of clubs. Seeing two honours on your left, you were going to cover? Careful! South may duck in dummy and pick up the rest of the suit by taking a marked finesse of the nine.

UNBLOCKING

The difficulty with unblocking plays is that often you must risk establishing an extra trick for the declarer. When in doubt about this, it is usually still right to unblock. Here the defender's problem is fairly simple:

```
                    ♠ A
                    ♡ K 9 5
                    ♢ A 6 3 2
                    ♣ A Q J 10 8
    ♠ K 9 7 6 5                       ♠ Q J 3
    ♡ Q 6 4 2      ┌─────────┐        ♡ J 8 7
    ♢ J 10         │ N       │        ♢ Q 9 8 7
    ♣ 6 3          │ W     E │        ♣ K 7 4
                   │     S   │
                   └─────────┘
                    ♠ 10 8 4 2
                    ♡ A 10 3
                    ♢ K 5 4
                    ♣ 9 5 2
```

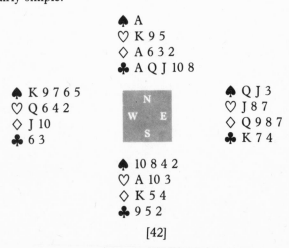

[42]

South plays in 3NT and West leads the six of spades to dummy's ace. There is no doubt here that East must unblock, playing the queen. It is true that this might cost a trick if South's spades were 10 9 x x, but East, holding the king of clubs, can see that the only chance for the defence is to run four tricks in spades. If his partner has K 10 x x x the unblock will not be necessary, but it is very necessary as the cards lie.

There are many similar situations. For example:

A

Q J 10 8 4 2   K 3

9 7 6 5

West leads the queen to dummy's ace. East should unblock, unless he can be sure that West has an outside entry that cannot be removed early on.

K

J 10 9 7 5 2   Q 4

A 8 6 3

If East can expect to win an early defensive trick he must throw the queen under dummy's king.

Sometimes it is right to unblock even when you can see that this will present the opponents with an easy trick.

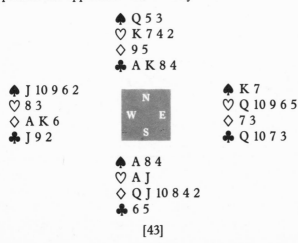

♠ Q 5 3
♡ K 7 4 2
◇ 9 5
♣ A K 8 4

♠ J 10 9 6 2
♡ 8 3
◇ A K 6
♣ J 9 2

♠ K 7
♡ Q 10 9 6 5
◇ 7 3
♣ Q 10 7 3

♠ A 8 4
♡ A J
◇ Q J 10 8 4 2
♣ 6 5

[43]

South is in 3NT and West leads the jack of spades. South plays low from dummy, and so long as East plays the king his side will easily defeat the contract. If East plays the seven, however, South will win with the ace and play on diamonds. West will win the second round and lead the ten of spades. If South takes the right view now, playing low from dummy, the spades will be blocked and the contract will be made.

LET IT WIN

There are many occasions in defence when it is unwise to take a trick that is offered. Consider this deal:

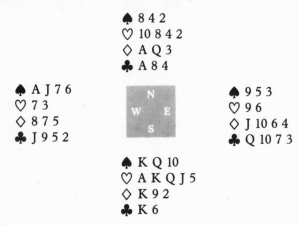

```
              ♠ 8 4 2
              ♡ 10 8 4 2
              ◇ A Q 3
              ♣ A 8 4
♠ A J 7 6                      ♠ 9 5 3
♡ 7 3            N             ♡ 9 6
◇ 8 7 5     W       E         ◇ J 10 6 4
♣ J 9 5 2        S             ♣ Q 10 7 3
              ♠ K Q 10
              ♡ A K Q J 5
              ◇ K 9 2
              ♣ K 6
```

South played in six hearts and West led a diamond. South drew trumps, ruffed the third round of clubs in his own hand, and played two more diamonds, finishing in dummy. A spade went to the king and ace; West then returned a spade into South's Q 10.

"Couldn't you let the king of spades hold?" demanded East.

"How could I do that? He might have held K x", West replied.

Yes, if South had dropped a card on the floor, but not otherwise. It was easy to count the South hand and to know that he held three spades.

West had the same sort of spade holding on the next deal. This time the play was rather more difficult.

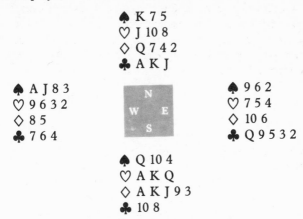

```
              ♠ K 7 5
              ♡ J 10 8
              ◇ Q 7 4 2
              ♣ A K J
♠ A J 8 3                          ♠ 9 6 2
♡ 9 6 3 2          N               ♡ 7 5 4
◇ 8 5          W       E           ◇ 10 6
♣ 7 6 4            S               ♣ Q 9 5 3 2
              ♠ Q 10 4
              ♡ A K Q
              ◇ A K J 9 3
              ♣ 10 8
```

Defending against six diamonds, West began with a trump. South took two rounds, then led a low spade. After shuffling round for a while, West went up with the ace and South had no further problems.

"I had to play the ace because you might have had a singleton", West explained. Then, gathering steam, he added: "Also, South might have had a doubleton spade with something like Q x of clubs. Then I might never make the ace".

The second point was certainly foolish. If South had held two spades and Q x of clubs, he would presumably have taken his discard right away. The first point might just have been sound—if the South hand had been precisely ♠ x ♡ A K Q ◇ A K J x x ♣ 10 x x x.

There is one other point worth mentioning. As the cards lay, South might have made the contract against any defence. Do you see how? After drawing trumps he can eliminate the hearts and clubs, then play a spade to the *queen*. This unlikely sequence would have forced West to win and return a spade, which would have run to the declarer's ten.

A defender playing in front of dummy's K J combination will often have a difficult decision whether or not to go up with his ace.

```
              ♠ J 4 3
              ♡ K J 9 4
              ◇ J 8 4
              ♣ 6 3 2
♠ 8 7 2                          ♠ 9 6
♡ A 10 7 3          N           ♡ Q 8 2
◇ 10 6          W       E       ◇ 9 7 3 2
♣ K Q J 9           S           ♣ A 10 7 4
              ♠ A K Q 10 5
              ♡ 6 5
              ◇ A K Q 5
              ♣ 8 5
```

South, who has bid both his suits, plays in four spades. Clubs are
led and the third round is ruffed. South draws two rounds of
trumps, then leads a low heart. West has to decide whether to take
the ace or to give declarer a chance to finesse.

A defender must be prepared for this kind of situation. A player
who ponders and then plays low is marked with the ace, since with
Q x x he would have nothing to think about. When it is impossible
to judge whether declarer has a singleton or a doubleton, it is
usually good play to duck. Declarer with a doubleton, and possibly
with a singleton, will tend to play the jack, thinking that if the
defender had held the ace he might have played it.

There is one more interesting point about the play, which you
may or may not have noticed. South led a low heart after just two
rounds of spades, leaving one spade at large. The reason for this was
that he did not want to give the defender with a doubleton spade a
chance to signal his length in another suit. Suppose that South had
drawn a third round of trumps: this would have given East a chance
to make an informative discard. A low card, such as the two of
hearts, would indicate an odd number in the suit; a high card, such
as the seven of diamonds, would be the beginning of a high-low
signal, showing an even number. Either discard would enable West
to judge his partner's complete distribution, since West already had
a count of the spades and clubs.

USE AN HONOUR TO KILL AN HONOUR

It is generally right to use an honour card to kill an opponent's honour card. In other words, it tends to be a mistake to play a high card on air. The point arises here in the spade suit.

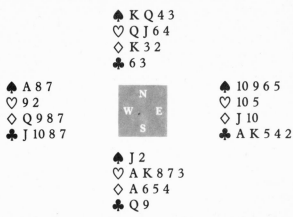

```
              ♠ K Q 4 3
              ♡ Q J 6 4
              ◇ K 3 2
              ♣ 6 3
 ♠ A 8 7                      ♠ 10 9 6 5
 ♡ 9 2            N           ♡ 10 5
 ◇ Q 9 8 7     W   E          ◇ J 10
 ♣ J 10 8 7       S           ♣ A K 5 4 2
              ♠ J 2
              ♡ A K 8 7 3
              ◇ A 6 5 4
              ♣ Q 9
```

South opens one heart and North raises to four hearts. West leads the jack of clubs, and after cashing two club tricks East exits with the jack of diamonds. South draws trumps, then leads a low spade. It would be poor play now to go up with the ace, enabling South later to discard two diamonds on ♠ K Q. Equally, if South led the jack of spades from hand, it would be essential to kill this card by playing the ace.

3

In dummy play

AVOIDING AN OVERRUFF

When you play a crossruffing type of game it is usually correct to
ruff low early on and to ruff with high trumps later. If you have
enough good trumps to ruff high all the time, so much the better.

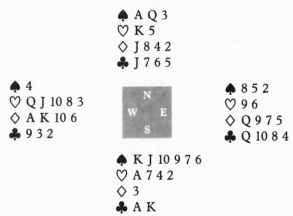

♠ A Q 3
♡ K 5
◇ J 8 4 2
♣ J 7 6 5

♠ 4
♡ Q J 10 8 3
◇ A K 10 6
♣ 9 3 2

♠ 8 5 2
♡ 9 6
◇ Q 9 7 5
♣ Q 10 8 4

♠ K J 10 9 7 6
♡ A 7 4 2
◇ 3
♣ A K

After one spade—three spades South, quite reasonably, advanced
to six spades. The defence began with two rounds of diamonds,
South ruffing with the spade six. After prolonged thought the
declarer cashed ace and king of clubs, crossed to the queen of
spades, and ruffed a club with the seven of spades. Having failed to
bring down the queen, he needed two heart ruffs. He had to ruff low
on the third round and was overruffed. East returned a trump and
South finished two down.

"That was very unlucky," South informed the table. "If the
queen of clubs comes down in three rounds I need only one heart
ruff."

Even that was not an accurate analysis. If the queen of clubs comes down in three rounds, declarer needs to ruff a heart and find the trumps 2–2, so that he can cash the established jack of clubs.

There was another way to lose the contract. South might have set about the hearts immediately and ruffed the third round with a low trump. The correct play is very simple. South should begin by cashing two hearts. When these stand up, he can ruff two hearts with the ace and queen of spades, taking no risk at all.

WHY FINESSE?

Poor players like to take a finesse and are both proud and happy when the play succeeds. Good players don't like to finesse at all; they look for some surer way of making the extra trick.

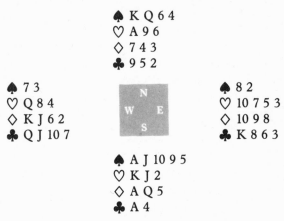

```
                    ♠ K Q 6 4
                    ♡ A 9 6
                    ◇ 7 4 3
                    ♣ 9 5 2
   ♠ 7 3                              ♠ 8 2
   ♡ Q 8 4            N               ♡ 10 7 5 3
   ◇ K J 6 2       W     E            ◇ 10 9 8
   ♣ Q J 10 7         S               ♣ K 8 6 3
                    ♠ A J 10 9 5
                    ♡ K J 2
                    ◇ A Q 5
                    ♣ A 4
```

South is in four spades and West leads the queen of clubs. Declarer lets West hold the first trick, wins the second, and plays a trump to the queen. It is good play now to eliminate the third club by ruffing with the jack. Then a spade to the king draws the outstanding trumps.

The diamond finesse can hardly be avoided, so South plays a low diamond to the queen and king. Having noted his partner's ten of diamonds, West exits with a diamond to the eight and ace. The position is now:

[49]

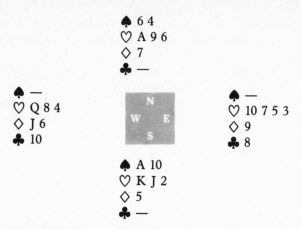

Instead of taking a straightforward heart finesse, South exits with his losing diamond. East wins and must lead a low heart. South plays low and West has to contribute the queen.

Note that by following this sequence the declarer doubled his chances of not losing a heart. He would have gone down only if East had been able to win the third diamond and West had held both queen and ten of hearts. You see the importance of ruffing the third club? If this is not done, the defenders can exit in clubs instead of opening up the hearts.

This is another example of elimination play, as it is called:

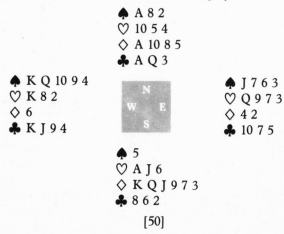

The easiest contract for North-South is 3NT, but suppose South becomes the declarer in five diamonds, after West has overcalled in spades.

South wins the spade lead with the ace and, as a matter of ordinary technique, ruffs a spade at trick two. After drawing trumps in two rounds he eliminates dummy's third spade, arriving at this position:

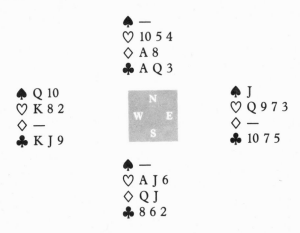

♠ —
♡ 10 5 4
◇ A 8
♣ A Q 3

♠ Q 10
♡ K 8 2
◇ —
♣ K J 9

♠ J
♡ Q 9 7 3
◇ —
♣ 10 7 5

♠ —
♡ A J 6
◇ Q J
♣ 8 6 2

South finesses the queen of clubs, then plays ace and another. The effect of this is that, whether East or West wins the third club, the defenders are forced either to lead a spade, conceding a ruff-and-discard, or a heart; and however the hearts lie, South will lose only one trick in the suit.

In case you doubt that, suppose the heart distribution had been:

10 5 4

K Q 3   9 8 7 2

A J 6

Even if East had been on lead, the defence would have made only one trick in hearts. West would have won the first round but would then have been 'on play', as it is called, forced to concede a ruff-and-discard or to return a heart.

WHEN NOT TO DRAW TRUMPS

On many hands the declarer must make sure of ruffing losers before he draws trumps.

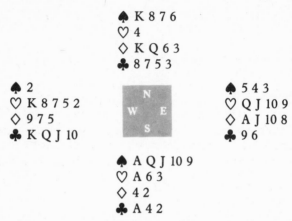

```
                    ♠ K 8 7 6
                    ♡ 4
                    ◇ K Q 6 3
                    ♣ 8 7 5 3
  ♠ 2                                ♠ 5 4 3
  ♡ K 8 7 5 2          N            ♡ Q J 10 9
  ◇ 9 7 5          W       E        ◇ A J 10 8
  ♣ K Q J 10          S             ♣ 9 6
                    ♠ A Q J 10 9
                    ♡ A 6 3
                    ◇ 4 2
                    ♣ A 4 2
```

South is in four spades and West leads the king of clubs. South wins and must not, on this occasion, draw trumps. If he does so, and nothing else goes right, he will find himself losing two clubs, a heart and a diamond. Instead, South should play ace and another heart, return to hand with a trump, and ruff the last heart. He makes his contract for the loss of two clubs and one diamond.

Another time when it would be wrong to draw trumps is when an early discard is needed and declarer must not risk losing the lead.

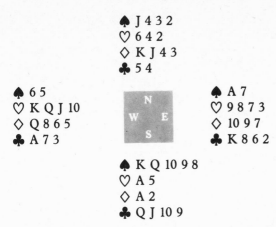

```
              ♠ J 4 3 2
              ♡ 6 4 2
              ◇ K J 4 3
              ♣ 5 4
♠ 6 5                        ♠ A 7
♡ K Q J 10         N        ♡ 9 8 7 3
◇ Q 8 6 5      W       E    ◇ 10 9 7
♣ A 7 3            S         ♣ K 8 6 2
              ♠ K Q 10 9 8
              ♡ A 5
              ◇ A 2
              ♣ Q J 10 9
```

West leads the king of hearts against South's contract of four spades. If South plays a round of trumps he will surely lose a spade, a heart and two clubs. It is right to try the diamond finesse, in the hope of cashing the king of diamonds and discarding the heart loser.

REFUSING TO RUFF

Sometimes the declarer must refuse to ruff an opponent's winner because it would be dangerous to shorten his own trumps. This is called "discarding a loser on a loser".

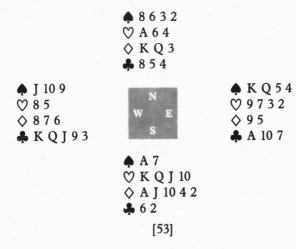

```
              ♠ 8 6 3 2
              ♡ A 6 4
              ◇ K Q 3
              ♣ 8 5 4
♠ J 10 9                     ♠ K Q 5 4
♡ 8 5              N        ♡ 9 7 3 2
◇ 8 7 6       W       E     ◇ 9 5
♣ K Q J 9 3       S         ♣ A 10 7
              ♠ A 7
              ♡ K Q J 10
              ◇ A J 10 4 2
              ♣ 6 2
```

[53]

South plays in a delicate contract of four hearts and the defence begins with three rounds of clubs. If declarer ruffs and tries to draw trumps, East will ruff the third diamond and make a spade in due course. It is better play for South to discard a spade on the third round of clubs. The rest of the hand then presents no problem.

Sometimes it is better to play loser on loser even when there is no shortage of trumps. Here South plays in five clubs.

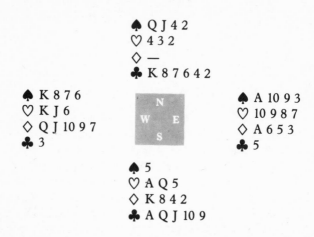

```
              ♠ Q J 4 2
              ♡ 4 3 2
              ◇ —
              ♣ K 8 7 6 4 2
♠ K 8 7 6                          ♠ A 10 9 3
♡ K J 6          N                 ♡ 10 9 8 7
◇ Q J 10 9 7   W   E               ◇ A 6 5 3
♣ 3              S                 ♣ 5
              ♠ 5
              ♡ A Q 5
              ◇ K 8 4 2
              ♣ A Q J 10 9
```

West leads the queen of diamonds. If South ruffs in dummy he will find it impossible, against reasonable defence, to avoid the loss of one spade and two hearts. The hand plays easily if at trick one the declarer discards a heart from dummy. Another heart goes later on the king of diamonds and South loses just one diamond and one spade.

DUCKING PLAY

All players who are not beginners are familiar with the simpler forms of ducking play. Sometimes it is necessary to duck twice in the same suit, and this tactical move is often missed.

```
              ♠ Q 5 2
              ♡ 7 4 2
              ◇ 4 3
              ♣ A K 7 3 2
♠ J 9 7          N          ♠ K 10 8 3
♡ 9 6         W     E       ♡ Q J 10 3
◇ 10 9 8 6       S          ◇ Q 7 5 2
♣ Q 10 8 4                  ♣ J
              ♠ A 6 4
              ♡ A K 8 5
              ◇ A K J
              ♣ 9 6 5
```

South plays in 3NT and West leads the ten of diamonds. Placing declarer with the top honours, East plays low and South wins with the jack. Seeing that at least one club must be lost, South ducks the first round to East's jack. As South has bid hearts, East returns his partner's suit, a diamond to the ace. South leads another low club and a shrewd West may play the queen. Declarer now puts on dummy's king, and suddenly the contract is in serious danger.

South could have afforded to duck another round of clubs, thus making sure of nine tricks.

PROTECTING HIGH CARDS

You are the declarer in a notrump contract and a suit is led in which you have a moderate guard, such as Q x in dummy, J x x in hand. You must play low from dummy, not the queen. Most players know that, but there are a few tricky situations in this area. For example:

```
                    ♠ K 5
                    ♡ 8 4 2
                    ◇ K Q 10 7 3
                    ♣ A J 8
♠ 6 led

                    ♠ J 7 4 2
                    ♡ K 7
                    ◇ A 8 5
                    ♣ K Q 6 4
```

You play in 3NT after West has overcalled in hearts. West leads the six of spades. Normally you would play low from dummy with this combination, making sure of one trick, but here you must do all you can to prevent East from gaining the lead and firing a heart through the king.

Another common holding is J x in dummy, A 10 x in hand. Here you can be sure of two tricks by playing low from dummy and heading East's king or queen with the ace. Still, there are occasions when it is right to hold up the ace. This occurs when West is unlikely to have a side entry.

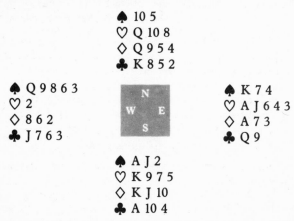

```
                    ♠ 10 5
                    ♡ Q 10 8
                    ◇ Q 9 5 4
                    ♣ K 8 5 2
♠ Q 9 8 6 3                          ♠ K 7 4
♡ 2              N                   ♡ A J 6 4 3
◇ 8 6 2        W   E                 ◇ A 7 3
♣ J 7 6 3        S                   ♣ Q 9
                    ♠ A J 2
                    ♡ K 9 7 5
                    ◇ K J 10
                    ♣ A 10 4
```

South plays in 3NT after East has opened one heart. West decides to lead a spade; dummy plays low and East the king. Now South must not, from force of habit, put on the ace. Suppose he does this and forces out the ace of diamonds. East will lead a second spade, which West will duck, and South will then be forced to concede three spades and two aces.

Since East opened one heart, South knows that the two aces are on his right. He must hold up the ace of spades until the third round. All he need lose then is two spades and two aces.

This is another deal where the declarer must play carefully to protect his high cards in the suit led:

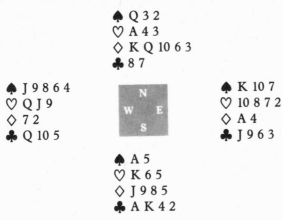

♠ Q 3 2
♡ A 4 3
◇ K Q 10 6 3
♣ 8 7

♠ J 9 8 6 4
♡ Q J 9
◇ 7 2
♣ Q 10 5

♠ K 10 7
♡ 10 8 7 2
◇ A 4
♣ J 9 6 3

♠ A 5
♡ K 6 5
◇ J 9 8 5
♣ A K 4 2

West leads the six of spades against 3NT. It would be wrong here to put in the queen because, if this is headed by the king, South will be able to hold up the ace for only one round. Evidently, he will lose four tricks in spades and the ace of diamonds.

South plays low from dummy, therefore, and East finesses the ten. As the cards lie, it would not be fatal to duck, but this is not the natural play. South should win with the ace and play on diamonds. His worries are over when East plays the ace. Suppose, at worst, that West held the ace of diamonds and followed with the jack of spades. South would have to decide then whether to play the queen or to play low, which would be best when East held K x x.

SAFETY PLAYS

There are innumerable situations in a single suit where one method of play is slightly better than another. We will look at just a few of these.

K 9 4 2

A Q 10 8 3

This one you surely know. You must start with the ace (or queen) so that you can pick up J x x x on either side.

K 7 4 2

A Q 9 5 3

This time you can pick up J 10 x x in the East hand, but not in the West hand. You must begin with the king therefore.

Q 8 3

A K 10 7 2

If you are short of entries to dummy, be sure to begin with a high card from hand. You follow with the two to the queen, and then, if West shows out, you can pick up East's J 9 x x.

K 7 5 3

A J 10

You need to make four tricks and have no clue to the lie of the queen. If entries permit, begin with a low card to the jack. Then you can pick up either Q x or Q x x x in the East hand without loss.

A K J 4

7 5 3

You need precisely three tricks. Play off the ace and king first—a safety play that will gain when East holds Q x. If nothing happens when you play off the top cards, return to hand to lead towards the J x.

J 7 4 2

A Q 9 6 5 3

It is usually right to lead a low card when about to finesse, but here the jack is best. You intend to finesse, and leading the jack enables you to pick up East's K 10 x without loss.

A J 7 5 4 2

Q 3

You can never make six tricks against good defence. To make five tricks, entries permitting, play low to the ace. A defender may hold the singleton king.

A Q 5 2

J 3

Don't lead the jack from hand (at notrumps). That way, you can never make more than two tricks. Best is to lead low from dummy towards the jack. If this holds, duck the next round. You will make three tricks when East holds K x or K x x.

As we said, there are many problems of this kind, and we will show some more later. It is excellent practice to take a single suit, deal anything from seven to ten cards to one side, and determine the best way to tackle the combination. In many cases the likely play of (imaginary) opponents will come into the reckoning. Are they likely to play false cards, and so forth?

KNOCK ON THE HEAD

There are many situations where the main object is to force opponents to play *their* high cards on *your* low ones. This is a simple example:

K Q 7 4 2

A J 5   9 8

10 6 3

You would begin with a low card to the queen. When this held, you would aim to return to hand for the next lead of the suit. The same sort of principle arises on this deal:

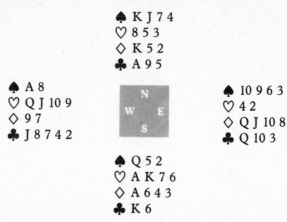

                    ♠ K J 7 4
                    ♡ 8 5 3
                    ◇ K 5 2
                    ♣ A 9 5

♠ A 8   ♠ 10 9 6 3
♡ Q J 10 9   N   ♡ 4 2
◇ 9 7   W   E   ◇ Q J 10 8
♣ J 8 7 4 2   S   ♣ Q 10 3

                    ♠ Q 5 2
                    ♡ A K 7 6
                    ◇ A 6 4 3
                    ♣ K 6

South plays in 3NT and West leads the queen of hearts. Declarer wins the first or second trick and leads a low spade to the jack, which holds. Now many players would return a spade to the queen and ace. From that point onwards it would be difficult to establish a ninth trick.

It costs nothing here to return to hand after the jack of spades and lead another low spade. This gains when West has a doubleton A x.

The diamond combination on the following hand occurs often:

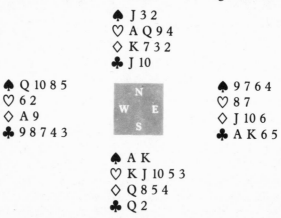

                    ♠ J 3 2
                    ♡ A Q 9 4
                    ◇ K 7 3 2
                    ♣ J 10

♠ Q 10 8 5   ♠ 9 7 6 4
♡ 6 2   N   ♡ 8 7
◇ A 9   W   E   ◇ J 10 6
♣ 9 8 7 4 3   S   ♣ A K 6 5

                    ♠ A K
                    ♡ K J 10 5 3
                    ◇ Q 8 5 4
                    ♣ Q 2

South is in four hearts and West leads the nine of clubs. After cashing two clubs East switches to the seven of spades.

[60]

South's problem is to avoid losing two tricks in diamonds. He can do this only if he can find an opponent with a doubleton ace of diamonds, and even then he must play the first diamond from the right hand. Since East has turned up with ace and king of clubs, it is fair to assume that West holds the ace of diamonds. The declarer begins, therefore, with a low diamond to the king. He plays low from hand on the next round, bringing down West's ace.

DEVELOP OR FINESSE?

Sometimes the declarer will have a chance to win an extra trick either by establishing a winner or by finessing. If entries permit, it will usually be right to try first to develop a trick by force.

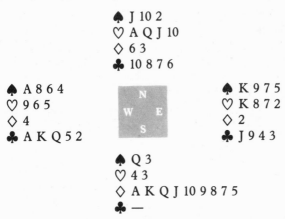

```
                    ♠ J 10 2
                    ♡ A Q J 10
                    ◊ 6 3
                    ♣ 10 8 7 6
♠ A 8 6 4                            ♠ K 9 7 5
♡ 9 6 5           N                  ♡ K 8 7 2
◊ 4             W   E                 ◊ 2
♣ A K Q 5 2        S                  ♣ J 9 4 3
                    ♠ Q 3
                    ♡ 4 3
                    ◊ A K Q J 10 9 8 7 5
                    ♣ —
```

South opens five diamonds and all pass. West leads the king of clubs. South ruffs and draws trumps.

If declarer could find West with the king of hearts he would make at least one overtrick, but the chance of establishing a spade winner must not be overlooked. Don't enter dummy and lead a low spade to the queen: instead, put pressure on West by leading a low spade from hand. There is many a player in the West position who would fail to go up with the ace. If West plays low, the defence is lost.

[61]

WHEN THERE IS A CHOICE OF FINESSES

Everyone is familiar with this combination of honours:

6 4 2

A J 10

Initially, what do you think are the chances of making two tricks from this combination? If you are a betting man you will recognize that you have a 3 to 1 on chance: you fail only if West has both king and queen.

Suppose, however, that the first finesse has lost to the king or queen. What do you suppose now are the chances of the second finesse succeeding?

This is not, as you might think, an even chance. The fact that West has captured the first trick with the king (or queen) affords a presumption that he does *not* hold the queen (or king). It is about two to one on that the second finesse will succeed. Consider, in this light, the play on the following deal:

♠ K J 5
♡ K 10 9 6
◇ 8 6 4
♣ A 6 2

♠ A Q 8 6 4 3
♡ 8 3 2
◇ K Q J
♣ 3

South plays in four spades and the defence begins with ace and another diamond. Trumps are drawn in three rounds and all will depend on whether South loses two, or three, tricks in hearts.

You would no doubt begin by finessing the nine or ten. East wins with the jack (or queen) and when you lead the next heart West again plays low.

It is not now an even choice whether you should go up with the king or finesse again. The fact that East has won the first heart with the jack (or queen) affords a presumption that he does *not* hold the queen (or jack).

Note that the same kind of argument cannot be applied to this combination:

A Q 10

4 3 2

You begin with a finesse of the ten, and this loses to the jack. This tells you nothing about the position of the king. The second finesse is (almost exactly) an even chance.

See if the earlier discussion helps you to find the best line on this deal:

♠ A K 10 8
♥ 7 6 4 2
♦ A 3
♣ K 8 4

♠ 9 5
♥ A Q 5
♦ K 4
♣ A Q J 10 7 2

You play in six clubs and West leads the queen of diamonds. You win with the king and draw trumps in three rounds. How do you continue?

One possibility is to play ace, king and another spade, with a faint chance of bringing down the queen and jack in three rounds. If this fails, you will need the heart finesse.

However, there is a stronger line. After drawing trumps lead a low spade to the eight. This will probably lose to the queen or jack and East will lead a heart. Now go up with the ace and take the second finesse in spades. You will look a little foolish if East holds Q J of spades and also the king of hearts, but that's life!

ESTABLISH THE SUIT

As we remarked earlier, the finesse is usually the last string in the declarer's bow. Two finesses are offered on this next deal, but neither should be taken.

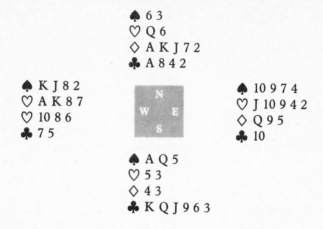

```
                    ♠ 6 3
                    ♡ Q 6
                    ◇ A K J 7 2
                    ♣ A 8 4 2
  ♠ K J 8 2                          ♠ 10 9 7 4
  ♡ A K 8 7            N             ♡ J 10 9 4 2
  ♡ 10 8 6         W       E         ◇ Q 9 5
  ♣ 7 5               S             ♣ 10
                    ♠ A Q 5
                    ♡ 5 3
                    ◇ 4 3
                    ♣ K Q J 9 6 3
```

South opens one club and West passes. What would you respond on the North hand? Three clubs is not forcing in most systems, so you should cross that out. Most modern players would respond simply one diamond, but this may cause problems on the next round. We favour an old-fashioned two diamonds. South rebids three clubs and now North jumps to five clubs. This conveys the inference that North does not possess first or second round control of either of the unbid suits.

West cashes two top hearts and switches to a trump. South should look ahead before deciding whether it would be right to draw a second round. If he needed to set up just one trick in diamonds, ruffing twice if necessary, he would retain the extra entry in trumps, but on this occasion his object is to establish two diamond winners. He can afford to draw the outstanding trump. Then three rounds of diamonds, as the cards lie, establish two winners for spade discards.

South was not dependent on finding the diamonds 3–3. He might have brought down a doubleton queen, which would be good enough. If the diamonds proved disappointing, an opponent holding such as Q 10 x x, then South would still be able to cross to dummy and finesse the queen of spades.

WHEN TO PLAY THE HIGH CARD FIRST

Suppose you hold this type of trump combination:

8 6 4

A K J 5 2

Would you begin with a finesse of the jack or would you lay down the ace first? This is a fairly easy question. Normally you should play the ace or king first, because of the possibility of finding West with a singleton queen. But suppose you were in dummy, perhaps for the last time: then it would be right to finesse the jack rather than play West for a singleton or doubleton queen.

Many combinations of this kind are deceptive. For example:

5 4 2

A Q J 7 3

Suppose you could afford to lose one trick in the suit, but not two. There is a slight advantage now in laying down the ace first. This will save the ship when West holds a singleton king. Of course, this type of play is right only when there are at least two entries to the opposite hand. West may hold a low singleton, East K 10 x x; in this case you will need to cross to dummy twice more.

A J 5 4 3

Q 6 2

If you need five tricks you must lead low and finesse the jack, playing West for K x. But suppose you need only four tricks? Then ace first is right, to guard against a singleton king in the East hand.

A K J 10 4

6 3

The best play for five tricks is to finesse on the first round. This will be good enough when West holds Q x x x. Playing the ace first can never gain, unless you propose to follow with the king, playing East for a doubleton queen. Suppose you need just four tricks from this combination. Again, it is right to finesse on the first round.

Playing the ace, with the intention of finessing later, will gain only when East has a singleton queen.

Q J 7 4 2

A 9 5 3

This combination is a little tricky. Say that you can afford to lose one trick, but not two. The right play is low from hand towards the Q J. If you make the normal play of queen first you won't be able to pick up West's K 10 8 6, and if you start by laying down the ace you will lose two tricks when East holds the four outstanding cards.

WHICH SUIT FIRST?

"Do you know, we had 24 points between us", exclaimed South after going one down in a contract of 1NT. As you may imagine, he hadn't played it very well.

```
                    ♠ A 8 5
                    ♡ 6 5 2
                    ◇ 10 6 4 3
                    ♣ K 7 2
  ♠ J 9 7 4 3          N          ♠ K 6
  ♡ K 9          W         E       ♡ A 10 8 4 3
  ◇ K J 5             S           ◇ 9 7
  ♣ 10 5 4                        ♣ J 8 6 3
                    ♠ Q 10 2
                    ♡ Q J 7
                    ◇ A Q 8 2
                    ♣ A Q 9
```

South opened 1NT and all passed. West led a low spade, won by the king, and East returned a spade. South took the trick in dummy and finessed the queen of diamonds. This lost and West cleared the spades, producing the following position:

[66]

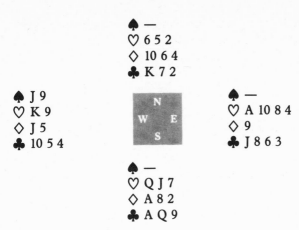

```
              ♠ —
              ♡ 6 5 2
              ◇ 10 6 4
              ♣ K 7 2
♠ J 9                        ♠ —
♡ K 9          N             ♡ A 10 8 4
◇ J 5       W     E          ◇ 9
♣ 10 5 4       S             ♣ J 8 6 3
              ♠ —
              ♡ Q J 7
              ◇ A 8 2
              ♣ A Q 9
```

South realized now that the contract was in some danger. He thought of crossing to the king of clubs and leading a heart to the queen, but two more spades from West would force him to bare the ace of diamonds. Finally he played ace and another diamond and lost seven tricks—three spades, two hearts and two diamonds.

Had South been in 3NT, or even in 2NT, his play would have been sound. Playing in 1NT, he should have looked for the safest way to develop a seventh trick. This, surely, was to lead twice towards the Q J of hearts. The odds against West holding both ace and king were mathematically 3 to 1—more in practice because with no high honour in hearts East might well have led this suit at trick two.

This is another deal where the declarer may play on the wrong suit:

```
              ♠ Q 10 6 4
              ♡ A 6
              ◇ K 8 5
              ♣ Q 10 7 3

              ♠ K 7 3
              ♡ Q 10 5
              ◇ A Q 4
              ♣ J 9 5 2
```

Playing a weak notrump, South opens 1NT, North raises to 2NT, and South has no more to say. West leads the seven of hearts, which runs to the jack and queen. Now it may seem natural to play on clubs, but is that right? The hearts are probably 5–3, and you will almost surely lose three hearts, ace of spades and ace-king of clubs. You simply have not time to play on the clubs. You must lead a low spade to the king when in dummy at trick three, and you must hope to make three tricks in spades. You can do this if West holds A J x or J x x.

WHEN THERE IS AN ENTRY PROBLEM

Nobody likes to find himself in the wrong hand when the tricks are there on top. You might go down in this contract on one of your bad days.

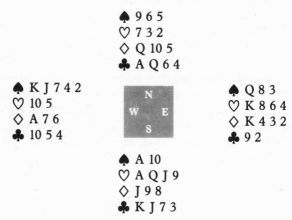

```
                    ♠ 9 6 5
                    ♡ 7 3 2
                    ◇ Q 10 5
                    ♣ A Q 6 4
   ♠ K J 7 4 2                      ♠ Q 8 3
   ♡ 10 5            N              ♡ K 8 6 4
   ◇ A 7 6       W       E          ◇ K 4 3 2
   ♣ 10 5 4          S              ♣ 9 2
                    ♠ A 10
                    ♡ A Q J 9
                    ◇ J 9 8
                    ♣ K J 7 3
```

Playing a 15–17 notrump, you open 1NT, North raises to 2NT, and you bid the game. West opens a low spade, finding your weakness. You win the second round and lead the jack of clubs, to which all follow.

The next card is important. You could play the king of clubs and overtake, as the cards lie, but clubs might be 4–1, so it is better to lead the seven (not the three) and win with the queen. A finesse of the queen of hearts wins. Now you play the king of clubs and overtake. When you play a heart to the jack, West drops the ten. You lead the three of clubs to dummy's six, and a finesse of the nine of hearts gives you game with four hearts, four clubs and the ace of spades.

Knowing the theme, you won't find this hand too difficult:

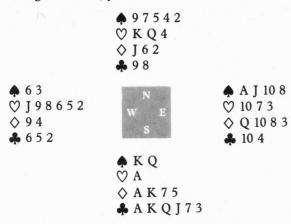

```
                  ♠ 9 7 5 4 2
                  ♡ K Q 4
                  ◇ J 6 2
                  ♣ 9 8
  ♠ 6 3                          ♠ A J 10 8
  ♡ J 9 8 6 5 2        N         ♡ 10 7 3
  ◇ 9 4            W       E      ◇ Q 10 8 3
  ♣ 6 5 2             S          ♣ 10 4
                  ♠ K Q
                  ♡ A
                  ◇ A K 7 5
                  ♣ A K Q J 7 3
```

South plays in five clubs and the defence begins with two rounds of spades. Some declarers would play off a string of clubs and lose two diamonds at the finish. The play is quite simple: cash the ace of hearts and follow with a low club. Ruff the next spade with a high trump, cross to the nine of clubs and discard two diamonds on the king-queen of hearts.

PART II

The Commonest Mistakes

4

In bidding

RESPONDING ON WEAK HANDS

A player who opens with a big bid, such as two clubs, can see his own cards: he wants to know what you, his partner, can contribute. Suppose you hold:

> ♠ 6 4
> ♡ 10 8 7 6 2
> ◇ 7 5
> ♣ J 8 6 3

Partner opens two clubs, you respond two diamonds, and the opener bids two spades. What now? You mustn't bid 2NT "because I had so little". Your side is already committed to game, so bid a cheerful three hearts. It might fit. In practice, the full deal was:

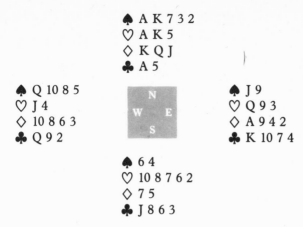

```
              ♠ A K 7 3 2
              ♡ A K 5
              ◇ K Q J
              ♣ A 5
♠ Q 10 8 5              ♠ J 9
♡ J 4         N        ♡ Q 9 3
◇ 10 8 6 3  W   E      ◇ A 9 4 2
♣ Q 9 2        S       ♣ K 10 7 4
              ♠ 6 4
              ♡ 10 8 7 6 2
              ◇ 7 5
              ♣ J 8 6 3
```

Four hearts can be made for the loss of one diamond, one club and one heart.

The situation is not quite the same when partner has opened with an Acol two bid, forcing for one round. This opening suggests playing strength plus honour strength, in that order. Suppose the bidding goes:

South	North
2♡	2NT
3◇	?

North holds:

```
♠ 10 8 7 6 2
♡ 6 4
◇ 7 5
♣ J 8 6 3
```

It would be a mistake now to introduce the weak spades, when partner is known to have two good suits. Just return to three hearts, which is not forcing in the system.

So the principle is this: when partner has opened two clubs or 2NT he has strength in various places and wants to know about your long suits. When he opens with an Acol two bid he is more interested in your support for his suits.

[71]

Whether it pays to play a weak notrump throughout, or a fairly strong notrump throughout, or to vary according to vulnerability and position at the table, is a debatable subject at all levels of play. It is advisable to be prepared for either method.

One of the advantages of playing a 15–17 notrumps is that you can open 1NT on hands such as that held by South on the following deal:

♠ 5 4 2
♡ Q J 5
◇ K 6 4
♣ K 6 5 3

♠ A Q
♡ K 10 2
◇ A Q J 3 2
♣ J 9 2

If you open one diamond partner will respond 1NT and you will finish in 3NT, played by North. This could easily fail against a spade lead, whereas 3NT by South has an excellent chance.

It is true that if you play a weak notrump of 12 to 14 points you will be able to open 1NT much more often, since hands of this range are commoner than hands in the 15–17 range. However, when the hand is weaker the advantage of being declarer in a notrump contract is less.

On the whole, and if the choice is yours, we advise a weak notrump not vulnerable and a strong notrump vulnerable. It is true that the general tendency among tournament players is to play a weak notrump throughout, but (a) the scoring is different, and (b) good partnership understanding is necessary when responder is weak and a penalty is threatened.

RESPONDING TO 1NT ON WEAK HANDS

A simple take-out of 1NT into two of a suit is generally played as a weak response. Some interesting problems arise in this area. For example, partner opens a weak notrump and you hold:

♠ 7 4
♡ Q 8 6 4 3
◇ 9 5
♣ Q 6 4 2

Do you pass or bid two hearts (which of course is non-forcing)?

Most players would bid two hearts without any reflection. Now it is true that you are more likely to escape for one or two down in two hearts than in 1NT, but that is not the sole consideration. For one thing, if you are doubled in 1NT you can always retreat to two hearts. More important is the fact that a pass of 1NT often *sounds* stronger than a weakness response. If the strength among the other three players is equally divided, fourth hand may suspect that you are lurking with a fair hand not quite good enough for a raise.

On the other hand, if you bid two hearts, and this is followed by two passes, the player on your right may step in with a double or perhaps two spades.

Suppose, next, that you are playing transfer responses, whereby a response of two diamonds would command partner to rebid two hearts. (This is a common style in tournament play.) Now the rebid of two hearts will run to the player on your left, and he will be more likely to reopen than if you had passed 1NT.

The situation is a little different when your weak suit is spades. Partner opens a weak notrump, the next player passes, and you hold:

♠ J 9 6 4 2
♡ 8 7 4
◇ Q 7 5 4
♣ 3

Now it is right to bid two spades (or two hearts if you are playing transfer responses), because it will be more hazardous for the opponents to compete.

A response of two clubs, Stayman, may sometimes be enlisted to avert a likely disaster. Partner opens a weak notrump, the next player passes, and you hold:

♠ 8 4 3 2
♡ J 9 8
◇ J 7 3 2
♣ 6 4

If you pass, you are almost certain to run into a penalty. You may find it difficult to settle in your best suit after fourth hand has doubled. It is better here to take the bull by the horns and respond two clubs. Note that this stratagem is sound only when your hand is playable in spades, hearts and diamonds.

DEFENCE AGAINST PRE-EMPTIVE OPENINGS

West opens three hearts, your partner doubles, and East passes. What do you understand by the double?

Various schemes of defence against pre-empts have been tried at different times, but nowadays, both in tournament and rubber bridge, the normal action is to use double for take-out. The double in this position is sometimes called an "optional double", but this term is really a misnomer. When a partner says "optional doubles" he means that he plays double for take-out, though responder to the double may of course decide to pass.

Sometimes the decision may seem close between a double and a bid of one's long suit at the three level. Look at the South hand below. East opens three clubs. Would you bid three spades or would you double?

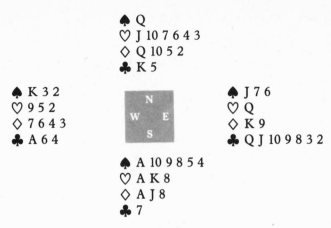

```
                    ♠ Q
                    ♡ J 10 7 6 4 3
                    ◇ Q 10 5 2
                    ♣ K 5
♠ K 3 2                              ♠ J 7 6
♡ 9 5 2          N                   ♡ Q
◇ 7 6 4 3      W   E                 ◇ K 9
♣ A 6 4          S                   ♣ Q J 10 9 8 3 2
                    ♠ A 10 9 8 5 4
                    ♡ A K 8
                    ◇ A J 8
                    ♣ 7
```

Although he has a good suit of spades, South should certainly double on his strong hand. North should jump to four hearts and South will probably pass. With the cards lying well, North can make twelve tricks in hearts. If South had overcalled in spades, North would have had to pass.

When an opponent opens with a pre-empt at the four level, it is usual to follow this scheme:

Double of four clubs or four diamonds is primarily for take-out.

Double of four hearts is primarily for penalties, but the doubler should be able to stand a take-out into four spades. Thus a responder to the double with such as

♠ Q 9 7 6 4 2   ♡ —   ◇ K 8 4 2   ♣ 7 4 3

should take out into four spades.

Double of four spades is primarily for penalties.

4NT is always for take-out. The player on your right opens four spades and you hold:

♠ —
♡ A Q J 3
◇ A K 9 5
♣ K Q 7 6 3

You overcall with 4NT. But be careful not to bid this hand twice. If partner responds in any suit at the five level you must pass.

[75]

It is sometimes said that when your partner opens with a pre-emptive three bid you need the values of an opening bid before you can raise to game. That is a *very* poor summary. You need more than a minimum opening, and you need *aces*. In this area one ace is better holding than two kings, because players who open with a three bid tend to hold singletons, and even if this is not the case the kings may not be worth a trick.

This type of hand often leads to an unnecessary penalty:

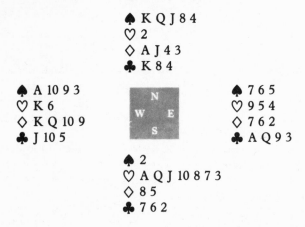

♠ K Q J 8 4
♡ 2
◇ A J 4 3
♣ K 8 4

♠ A 10 9 3
♡ K 6
◇ K Q 10 9
♣ J 10 5

♠ 7 6 5
♡ 9 5 4
◇ 7 6 2
♣ A Q 9 3

♠ 2
♡ A Q J 10 8 7 3
◇ 8 5
♣ 7 6 2

South opens three hearts—no-one could complain of that—and West passes. North has 14 points, but he has not enough *tricks* to consider 3NT or three spades (forcing) or four hearts. As you can see, there are six losers in a heart contract!

Changing the subject a little, suppose your partner has opened three hearts and you hold a stronger hand than the one above, something like:

♠ K Q J 8
♡ 2
◇ A Q 8 4
♣ A K 3 2

What would you say now? The right bid is four hearts—not 3NT, which (among good players) would say "I have heard your bid and I know the sort of hand you hold, but I have (perhaps) a solid minor and I want to play in 3NT, not in your suit."

OPENING 3NT AND RESPONSES

An opening bid of 3NT is a tactical move, usually based on a long minor suit. In the Acol system the opener (except in fourth hand) should hold not more than a queen outside a long solid suit. The bid is made on this type:

♠ 6
♡ 5 3
♢ J 6 3
♣ A K Q J 9 7 5

Some players may use the bid on a rather different type, such as:

♠ J 2
♡ Q 4
♢ A K Q J 6 5 4
♣ K 10

The first idea is better. On the second hand you can open one diamond.

The responses to the Acol type are based on tactical considerations. With a hand such as

♠ A 5 4 3   ♡ A 8 4 2   ♢ 5 3 2   ♣ Q 6

you know that partner's suit is diamonds and that the clubs are wide open, but perhaps they won't lead a club; anyway, you will take your chance on making 3NT. Also, if you are not vulnerable, it may be a good move to pass on quite a weak hand.

Avoid at all costs a folly such as bidding four spades on:

♠ K J 10 7 4 2
♡ Q 5 4 2
♢ A 3
♣ 4

You have no chance of making four spades opposite a long string of clubs. You expect to go down in 3NT, but you may as well pass until doubled.

Suppose partner opens 3NT, vulnerable, and you hold:

♠ A Q 8 6 3
♥ J 4
♦ 7 3
♣ J 8 4 2

You mustn't leave partner to suffer in 3NT, which might go three or four down. His suit is probably diamonds, but you cannot be sure. Bid four clubs and let him transfer to diamonds if he wishes.

It is important, when you play this type of 3NT opening, to leave all decisions to the responding hand. He knows what you've got, you don't know what he's got. If you are doubled, don't panic.

WHEN YOU ARE STRONG IN THE OPPONENT'S SUIT

East, on your right, opens one spade at game all and you hold:

♠ K Q 10 9 7
♥ A J 3
♦ A Q 3
♣ 5 2

What do you do? Pass (with or without a small trance)? Bid 1NT? Double? *Two* spades with contemptuous look?

All these things happen at rubber bridge, as surely you are aware. Let's cross out the bad selections first.

Two spades is amateurish, of course; it would imply anything but what you have—long spades. You might double and bid two spades on the next round. This sequence, unfortunately, would not express your hand. In the modern style it would say, "Tell me more".

1NT would not be a mistake, but it does not represent your best chance of obtaining a good result.

The correct action is to pass. If the player on your left responds, say, 1NT, and this is followed by two passes, you can double. Sometimes you will have a chance to double two spades for penalties.

That is what happened at the table when the full hand was:

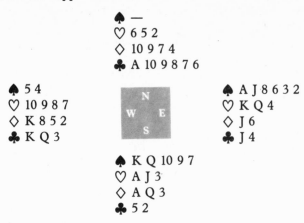

```
                    ♠ —
                    ♡ 6 5 2
                    ◇ 10 9 7 4
                    ♣ A 10 9 8 7 6
♠ 5 4                              ♠ A J 8 6 3 2
♡ 10 9 8 7          N              ♡ K Q 4
◇ K 8 5 2      W        E          ◇ J 6
♣ K Q 3            S               ♣ J 4
                    ♠ K Q 10 9 7
                    ♡ A J 3
                    ◇ A Q 3
                    ♣ 5 2
```

The bidding went:

South	West	North	East
—	—	—	1♠
No	1NT	No	2♠
Dble	No	No	No

Give North a good mark for passing the double and not removing it to three clubs. He held an ace and he assumed that his partner knew what he was doing. South led a club and the defenders easily won seven tricks, for a penalty of 500.

THE DOUBLE OF 1NT

The player on your left opens 1NT, your partner doubles and the next player passes. You hold:

```
♠ J 7 4 2
♡ 10 5 4
◇ 9 6 3
♣ 7 5 2
```

Seeking to gain time, you may perhaps inquire whether your opponents are playing a weak or a strong notrump. It makes no difference. The double of 1NT is a penalty double and you must pass. It is true that they may make the contract, but two spades by your side might well be a worse disaster. And for all you know, partner may be able to beat 1NT without any help from you.

The only time when it is sensible to remove a double of 1NT is when you hold a weak hand with a long suit, such as:

♠ 6   ♡ 10 4   ◇ J 8 6 5 3 2   ♣ 10 8 5 3

It is reasonable now to take out the double into two diamonds. But if your partner removes this to two spades, you mustn't blunder on with three diamonds or three clubs. He will probably hold at least K Q J 9 x x of spades and a couple of tricks in the side suits.

It follows that it is unwise to double 1NT unless you can cope with a weak hand opposite. Say that South opens a 12–14 notrump and you hold:

♠ A 7 5 4 2
♡ K J 8
◇ A Q
♣ J 5 2

It is, to say the least, dangerous to double. You propose to lead a spade against 1NT doubled, and if your partner is weak with short spades they will make at least one overtrick. It is very important to have a good lead when you are defending against 1NT.

Returning to the problems of the other defender, suppose that 1NT is doubled by your partner and you hold:

♠ 7 6 4
♡ A Q 8 5 3
◇ 4
♣ 9 7 6 3

It is "murder" to take out into two hearts. You may think "Partner won't lead a heart and my hand won't be much use to him." But that's not true; you will at least stop the opponents from making tricks in hearts and your side will certainly hold the balance of the cards.

[80]

Remember, then:

Don't double 1NT unless you can cope with a weak hand opposite.

Treat partner's double as a penalty double and don't spoil his fun.

RESCUE MANOEUVRES

When do you rescue partner's overcall, either before or after it has been doubled? It is an area where many horrible mistakes are made. Perhaps the best way to tackle it is to consider a number of examples and indicate whether, in our opinion, to rescue would be right, wrong, or debatable.

(1)	*South*	*West*	*North*	*East*
	—	1♠	2♡	No
	?			

You hold:

♠ J 6 4   ♡ —   ◇ K Q 10 8 6 4 3   ♣ 10 8 5

To rescue would be:

Wrong. In principle, one does not take out partner's overcall on weakness. Over three diamonds North might jump to four hearts. You pass for the moment, knowing that you may have a tricky decision later.

(2)	*South*	*West*	*North*	*East*
	—	1♠	2♡	Dble
	?			

You hold:

♠ J 6 4   ♡ —   ◇ K Q 10 8 6 4 3   ♣ 10 8 5

Whether you should rescue now is debatable. If the diamonds were a little better—say K Q J 9 x x—we would say yes, if they were worse we would say no. Remember you won't get any thanks if you take out into three diamonds and go three down—even if two hearts might also have been three down. Bear in mind always that when you raise the level of the bidding you benefit only if you can make *two* more tricks than partner would have made. If, in the present example, you make seven tricks in diamonds when he would have made six in hearts, the result is the same—two down.

(3) | South | West | North | East |
|---|---|---|---|
| — | 1◇ | 1♠ | Dble |
| ? | | | |

You hold:

♠ 4   ♡ Q 10 7 4   ◇ 9 6 3 2   ♣ 10 8 6 2

Here you *know* that one spade doubled will be bad, so to rescue is *right*. You might try 1NT for the moment, intending to redouble when this is doubled.

(4) | South | West | North | East |
|---|---|---|---|
| — | 1♠ | 1NT | Dble |
| ? | | | |

You hold:

♠ Q 5 2   ♡ 8 3   ◇ 10 7 6 4   ♣ Q 8 5 3

You have four points and may think that your side is not heavily outgunned. However, the weakness in hearts is a bad sign. With length in hearts partner would have doubled rather than overcall in notrumps. It is advisable to seek refuge in a minor suit. Two clubs would not be a mistake, but the more sophisticated action is to redouble. This is a rescue manoeuvre, because if you were content with 1NT doubled you would pass.

(5) | South | West | North | East |
|---|---|---|---|
| — | — | — | 1◇ |
| 2♣ | Dble | 2♠ | Dble |

You hold:

♠ —   ♡ A J 7 4 2   ◇ 9 5   ♣ K J 10 6 4 2

It would be wrong to rescue now, especially as you would be raising the level of the auction. Partner may well hold 6-2-4-1 distribution. East's double of two spades does not necessarily signify a strong trump holding.

(6) | *South* | *West* | *North* | *East* |
| --- | --- | --- | --- |
| — | 1♠ | 2NT | Dble |
| ? | | | |

You hold:

♠ J 10 7 5 4   ♡ A K 10 9 3 2   ◇ 5   ♣ 7

Both sides are vulnerable and partner's 2NT indicates a minor two-suiter. This problem was posed in a French magazine, and since the majority of the expert panelists voted for three hearts we must mark the problem as "debatable". Our own view is that three hearts is going to play badly even if partner has a doubleton, and that to pass the double of 2NT is at least as good. If partner has a strong minor suit, such as Q J 10 x x x, he may take out the double himself. If not, it should be possible to scramble a fair number of tricks, since the defenders will have no suit that they can run.

5

In defence

OPENING LEADS

The only rule one can lay down about opening leads is that there are
no rules. It is possible to make some general observations, of course,
but there will always be a host of exceptions. Perhaps the best way
to attack this subject is to examine some leads that are generally
wrong.

THE LEAD AT NOTRUMPS

At notrumps it is normally correct to lead your longest suit, but
there are two exceptions. First, a solid suit tends to be a better attack
than a broken suit. Here is a simple example:

```
                    ♠ K 5 2
                    ♡ A 7 5
                    ◇ K 10 8
                    ♣ 9 8 6 3

  ♠ Q J 10 8          N          ♠ 7 4 3
  ♡ J 4          W         E     ♡ Q 10 9 8
  ◇ Q 7 5 3 2         S          ◇ J 6
  ♣ 5 2                          ♣ A 10 7 4

                    ♠ A 9 6
                    ♡ K 6 3 2
                    ◇ A 9 4
                    ♣ K Q J
```

After 1NT–3NT West should prefer the queen of spades to a low diamond for at least two reasons: the spade is unlikely to give away a trick, and a lead of this suit is far more likely to establish winners than a diamond. On the present occasion the diamond attack immediately gives South a chance to establish his ninth trick in the suit led. A spade may not lead to more than one trick in the suit, but meanwhile South will have no good chance to arrive at nine winners.

The second point about the lead at notrumps is that the object is to attack not so much the long suit of the opening leader as the long suit of the partnership. That is why, with a weak hand, it is right to consider whether you will play for your own hand or for partner's. For example, after 1NT–3NT, you have to find a lead from:

♠ 7 4 2
♡ Q 5
♢ J 8 6 3 2
♣ 6 5 3

The chance of establishing diamond winners is very small because the suit is weak and your only possible side entry is the queen of hearts. It is natural, therefore, to attack one of the other suits, where your partner may have length, plus entries. Which side suit? Well, a major is more likely to find a weakness than a minor, so a spade is a better prospect than a club. The queen of hearts might turn out well, but this is a rather desperate shot. In general, it is better to lead from three cards than from a doubleton, because the lead from a doubleton will be strong only if partner holds five. And if you settle on a spade, which one? Conventionally, the seven, top of nothing, is correct, but with an intelligent partner the four or the two is a better choice. The point is that partner will know what is happening—he will know you are weak—and you should aim to conceal the general situation from the declarer.

LEADING A SINGLETON TRUMP

One of the few points on which all good players are agreed is that it is a mistake to lead a singleton trump except when it is clear that the declarer has a very strong holding. There is the danger that you may kill partner's Q x x, or that the deal will be something like this:

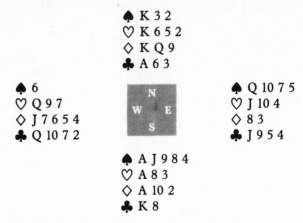

North opens with a strong notrump and South becomes declarer in six spades. Since a lead of any side suit *might* give up a trick, West will perhaps lead his singleton trump. This, as you can see, is fatal, because South will now lose no trump trick at all. Left to himself, he would certainly finesse the jack on the second round and so lose a spade and a heart.

The lead of a singleton trump is also liable to cost when partner holds a combination such as A J x, K J x, K 10 x x, and many others. On the present hand West should lead something like the seven of diamonds.

LEADING THE SINGLETON OF A SIDE SUIT

The best time to lead a singleton is when you hold a trump trick. Suppose the contract is four spades and you hold a singleton heart. If you hold something like A x or K x x of the trump suit, then your chance of obtaining a ruff is greatly improved: you will achieve this when partner has the ace of hearts and also when you can give him the lead in another suit after you have won a trump trick.

It is generally wrong to lead the singleton of a suit that has been bid by the declarer. It is all too likely now that you will kill a possible

trick in partner's hand, especially if he holds something like
Q 10 x x.

Sometimes you will have a choice between leading a singleton
and making a constructive lead such as the queen from Q J 9 x.
Either could be right, but in general—and especially if the
opponents have bid a side suit—we advise the more constructive
lead.

A special situation arises when you hold a singleton and four
trumps. Consider a hand such as this:

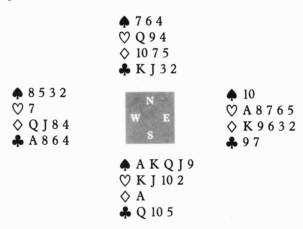

```
                    ♠ 7 6 4
                    ♡ Q 9 4
                    ◇ 10 7 5
                    ♣ K J 3 2
    ♠ 8 5 3 2                          ♠ 10
    ♡ 7                                ♡ A 8 7 6 5
    ◇ Q J 8 4                          ◇ K 9 6 3 2
    ♣ A 8 6 4                          ♣ 9 7
                    ♠ A K Q J 9
                    ♡ K J 10 2
                    ◇ A
                    ♣ Q 10 5
```

The bidding goes:

South	West	North	East
1♠	No	1NT	No
3♡	No	3♠	No
4♠	No	No	No

It would be wrong for West to lead his singleton heart for two
reasons: it might kill a likely trick in partner's hand, and in any case
the best chance for the defence lies in a forcing game.

As it happens, East holds the ace of hearts and can give his
partner a ruff. After that, the defence can make only the ace of
clubs.

Now study the effect of leading the queen of diamonds. South wins and draws trumps in four rounds. As soon as he touches hearts or clubs, the defenders win and force him to ruff with his last trump. South can make only nine tricks against best defence.

There are, however, two occasions when there is not much point in playing a forcing type of game. If the bidding indicates that the declarer is likely to hold six trumps, then a force will be effective only if the leader holds four trumps headed by a high honour. More important, suppose the bidding goes like this:

South	North
1◇	1♡
1♠	3♠
4♠	No

Now the trumps are likely to be 4–4, and if declarer is forced to ruff early on he will accept the force and play a crossruffing type of game. It is often good play, when you know the trumps are 4–4–4–1 round the table, to lead a trump. This is true when you hold a singleton trump as well as when you hold four.

THE LEAD FROM INDIVIDUAL HONOURS

Quite often, when the opponents have bid two suits, a defender has to decide whether to lead from K x x x or Q x x x, or perhaps from J x x x or 10 x x x of an unbid suit. Any of these leads may be fatal, but in general it is better to lead from a king than from any of the other single honours. This is because you may still make a trick even if partner has nothing in the suit.

When the choice is between Q x x x and J x x x, the low card from the queen tends to be better. As a rule, it will not cost if partner holds either the ace or king. A lead from an unsupported jack, on the other hand, tends to be bad in many situations.

The lead from an unsupported ten is deceptive. It is not constructive and it costs a trick more often than players realize. For example:

[88]

♠ K 10 9 4
♡ K J 9
♢ 8 3 2
♣ Q 10 4

♠ 8
♡ 10 5 4 2
♢ K J 9 4
♣ A 6 3 2

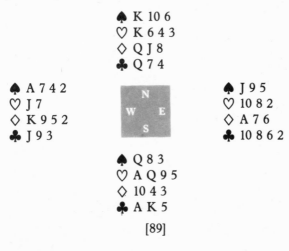

♠ 6 5 3
♡ Q 8 7
♢ A Q 10 6
♣ 9 7 5

♠ A Q J 7 2
♡ A 6 3
♢ 7 5
♣ K J 8

What is West to lead against four spades? A club would not cost as the cards lie, but it is not at all attractive. A singleton trump is always dangerous, as we mentioned above. As between hearts and diamonds, a diamond is certainly better. One example proves nothing, of course, but the heart, as you see, costs the vital trick.

WHEN TO LEAD AN ACE

As a rule, and unless you have length in the suit, leading an ace against a suit contract is almost as bad as *underleading* an ace. This is a very ordinary sort of deal:

♠ K 10 6
♡ K 6 4 3
♢ Q J 8
♣ Q 7 4

♠ A 7 4 2
♡ J 7
♢ K 9 5 2
♣ J 9 3

♠ J 9 5
♡ 10 8 2
♢ A 7 6
♣ 10 8 6 2

♠ Q 8 3
♡ A Q 9 5
♢ 10 4 3
♣ A K 5

[89]

West is on lead against four hearts. The only lead that gives the declarer a chance is a spade. On this occasion a low spade is better than the ace, because declarer may have to take a view on the second round, after he has headed the nine with the queen. This is another hand where any lead might be a mistake; we say only that the ace of spades is worse than any other.

Having made this point, let's consider a few situations where the lead of an unsupported ace could well be right.

1. When opponents have bid two suits strongly. The danger now is that if you make a neutral lead they will run too many tricks in their long suits. A lead from a hold such as A x x, normally very unfavourable, may now be right.

2. You have at least five cards in the suit, A x x x x. Now it is unlikely, though not impossible, that laying down the ace will cost a trick. One of the opponents may well have a singleton.

3. The lead of an ace from A x is sometimes a fair choice. Note here that you are less likely to be giving a trick than if you held A x x. (Declarer may lead low to the king or queen in dummy and duck the next round.) Sometimes the lead from A x will produce an early ruff.

4. A singleton ace is a problem. You have to consider whether there is any chance that you will be able to give partner the lead in another suit, enabling him to cash the king or give you a ruff. If this does not seem a realistic prospect, lead something else and hope that the ace will later kill an opponent's honour card.

THE LEAD FROM A DOUBLETON HONOUR

Suppose that, with no special indication about the side suits, you have to lead against four hearts from this holding:

♠ J 4
♡ 7 5
◇ A J 6 5 2
♣ A 8 5 2

Either ace might be a disaster. A trump might kill a queen in partner's hand. What about the jack of spades? This is the *worst* possible choice, killing a trick in many situations, notably when partner has an unsupported king or queen. The best choice, probably, is a trump, because even if partner holds Q x x there is no certainty that he would have made a trick. So, you lead from J x only when there seems no prospect in the other suits and partner might well hold something like K Q x x.

What about Q x? It is the same, really. Choose this only when it seems that this is the one suit where your side may be able to develop tricks.

It is not unreasonable, when your hand is *weak*, to lead from K x. This may turn out well in several ways. But don't make this lead when you have other good cards, because then the chance of finding partner with the ace is much less; and if partner has Q J x x you may be cut off from his hand after declarer has held up for one round.

We have already mentioned the possibility of leading the ace from A x. This is a fair "desperation shot" when the rest of your hand is weak.

THE LEAD FROM THREE OR FOUR SMALL

Suppose that opponents are in four spades and for a variety of possible reasons you decide to attack in an unbid suit where your holding is 7 4 2. Which card do you lead?

The traditional lead is the seven, described as "top of nothing". Many players would choose the four, known as MUD, because the intention is to follow the sequence of Middle, Up, Down. In America the normal practice is to lead the bottom card.

All these leads have certain disadvantages. If you lead the top card, the seven, partner doesn't know whether you hold two cards or three. Similarly, if you lead the four partner doesn't know whether you hold 4 2 or 7 4 2. And if you lead the two partner may not be able to tell whether you hold three small or something like Q x x.

In our opinion, the low card is unquestionably right. The MUD idea is absurd, really, because usually partner wants to know immediately whether you hold two cards or three. This is a typical situation:

Q 10 5 3

7 4 2   A K 9 6

J 8

West leads the four and East wins with the king. To play the ace now may be fatal, but of course, if West has led from 4 2, East must continue the suit. An opening lead of the two, on the other hand, puts East immediately in the picture.

It follows that if you are going to lead low from x x x you must not make the same lead from four cards. From a holding such as 9 7 5 3 the best choice is second from the top, the seven. Partner will always—well, nearly always—be able to judge whether you hold two cards or four.

THE LEAD FROM THREE OR FOUR TO AN HONOUR

It is normally correct, even in a suit contract, to lead low from three to an honour, whether partner has bid the suit or not. (The main exception is when you hold A x x in a suit contract.) This is because of situations such as:

(1)   6 5

Q 7 2   A 10 9 8 3

K J 4

(2)   6

J 8 4   A Q 9 7 2

K 10 5 3

It is clear, in both cases, that the lead of the high card will present declarer with an extra trick.

The conventional lead from four to an honour of partner's suit is fourth best, but there are many occasions where it is important for the opening leader, who has the weak hand, to retain the lead. For example:

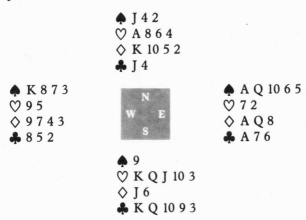

♠ J 4 2
♥ A 8 6 4
♦ K 10 5 2
♣ J 4

♠ K 8 7 3
♥ 9 5
♦ 9 7 4 3
♣ 8 5 2

♠ A Q 10 6 5
♥ 7 2
♦ A Q 8
♣ A 7 6

♠ 9
♥ K Q J 10 3
♦ J 6
♣ K Q 10 9 3

The bidding goes:

South	West	North	East
—	—	No	1♠
2♥	No	3♥	No
4♥	No	No	No

If West leads the three of spades the contract will be made, because South will discard three diamonds from dummy on his long clubs. Since West cannot expect ever to regain the lead if he begins with a low spade, he should lay down the king. Whether partner encourages or not, West must realize that the only chance now is to lead a diamond through the king.

LEADING FROM ACE-KING

In the club world it is still normal to lead the king from a suit such as A K x x x, and also, of course, the king from K Q 10 x x. In the tournament world most players lead the ace from a suit headed by A K, on the grounds that this enables a partner who holds, say, J x x to

[93]

distinguish. There is something in this, of course, but there are arguments the other way, too. If it is normal to lead the ace from suits headed by A K, what do you do when the best lead in your hand is the ace from A x x x x? We say only this: if you are happy leading the king from A K, there is no need to change.

There is, certainly, an advantage in what are known as Roman leads. In this style the *second* honour is always chosen—the king from A K, the queen from K Q, and so on. Another common practice in the tournament world is to define the ten as a strong lead, always promising a higher honour—queen, king or ace. The jack then signifies J 10 and others and denies a higher honour.

When your partner's lead indicates A K, it is correct to play the queen when you hold Q J alone or Q J and others. This is often a valuable scheme, because it enables the opening leader to follow with a low card on a deal such as this:

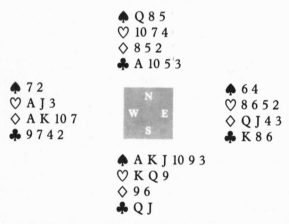

```
                    ♠ Q 8 5
                    ♡ 10 7 4
                    ◇ 8 5 2
                    ♣ A 10 5 3

♠ 7 2                                   ♠ 6 4
♡ A J 3              N                  ♡ 8 6 5 2
◇ A K 10 7      W         E             ◇ Q J 4 3
♣ 9 7 4 2           S                   ♣ K 8 6

                    ♠ A K J 10 9 3
                    ♡ K Q 9
                    ◇ 9 6
                    ♣ Q J
```

South is in three spades and West leads the king (or ace) of diamonds. When East plays the queen West knows that he can safely follow with the seven. East wins and switches to the eight of hearts, making it clear that he holds no honour. South plays the king, West ducks, and the defenders later take the king of clubs and two hearts to defeat the contract.

UNBLOCKING

We turn now to partner's play on the first trick, in particular to the times when it is right, or wrong, to unblock. East has a small problem on a deal of this type:

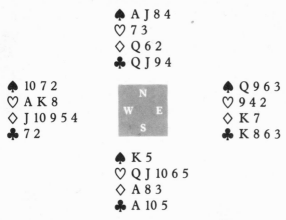

```
            ♠ A J 8 4
            ♡ 7 3
            ◇ Q 6 2
            ♣ Q J 9 4

♠ 10 7 2                    ♠ Q 9 6 3
♡ A K 8         N          ♡ 9 4 2
◇ J 10 9 5 4  W   E        ◇ K 7
♣ 7 2            S         ♣ K 8 6 3

            ♠ K 5
            ♡ Q J 10 6 5
            ◇ A 8 3
            ♣ A 10 5
```

South, who has opened one heart, plays in 3NT. West leads the jack of diamonds and declarer plays low from dummy. It would be wrong for East to play low, hoping later to kill the queen with the king. South would win and play on hearts. When West followed with the ten of diamonds South would probably play low from dummy, and the defence would then collapse.

East must hope that his partner has two entry cards. He unblocks the king of diamonds on the first trick. South will probably hold off and win the second round. Since West has both heart entries, the contract is sure to fail.

A defender who holds K x or Q x or J x must always be ready to unblock when a higher card is played in front of him. These are typical positions:

(1)   A 7 5

    Q 10 6 4 3   K 9

                       J 8 2

West leads the four against a notrump contract and declarer, hoping to block the run of the suit, plays the ace from dummy. East (unless he has no prospect of ever gaining the lead in another suit) must drop the king.

(2)   K 7 3

    J 10 6 5 3   Q 8

                          A 9 2

West leads the five and South, perhaps fearing a switch to another suit, wins with the king. East must certainly unblock, as he may otherwise be left with the queen on the next round of the suit.

(3)   K 7 3

    A 10 4   J 5

                          Q 9 8 6 2

In the middle of the play South leads low to the king. If it would be better for his partner to win the next trick in the suit, East must not fail to unload the jack.

A different type of unblocking play occurs when a defender holds a singleton ace or king in declarer's main suit.

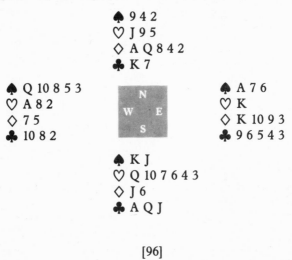

♠ 9 4 2
♥ J 9 5
♦ A Q 8 4 2
♣ K 7

♠ Q 10 8 5 3
♥ A 8 2
♦ 7 5
♣ 10 8 2

♠ A 7 6
♥ K
♦ K 10 9 3
♣ 9 6 5 4 3

♠ K J
♥ Q 10 7 6 4 3
♦ J 6
♣ A Q J

South is in four hearts and West leads a low spade, won by East. It may seem harmless to return a spade, but a good player in the South position will take advantage. He will cross to the king of clubs, ruff the third spade, cash two more clubs, and lead a trump. East will win with the king but will be "on play"—forced either to return a diamond or concede a ruff-and-discard. East can avert this calamity by cashing the king of hearts at trick two. This type of play would be easier, it is true, if East held a singleton ace of trumps rather than a singleton king.

SIGNALLING

Signalling is a tricky subject, if only because it falls into two parts: what signals should you include in your system, and when should you use them. Much depends on the relative strength of the players at the table. If you happen, in a pairs event, to run up against a top-ranking expert, it will probably be wise to exchange very few signals, because the declarer will deduce more from them than the defenders. On the other hand, it must be said that some very strong partnerships signal consistently, taking the view that the declarer has an initial advantage in reading the distribution and that the task of the defenders is to draw level, as it were.

It is, in any case, sensible to exchange signals early in the play, because at this point not much is known about the hand. Normally, a defender with a doubleton will play high-low on the first trick, but what do you think East should do in the following situation?

Q 9 7 5 3

A K 10 8 4   6 2

J

West, who has bid this suit, leads the king (or ace). As East, would you give a signal with the six, indicating an even number, or would you say to yourself, "I'll play the two; the last thing I want to do is encourage partner to play a second round."

It is impossible to do the right thing always in these positions, but in general East should give the standard distributional signal. Then, at least, if he plays the two partner will know it is a singleton.

Often a defender will have to decide whether to give a signal showing strength or a signal to show length. The general principle to follow is: Strength first, distribution second. In other words, if partner is going to be in any doubt about the lie of the high cards, clarify this for him. Consider what East should do in the following positions:

(1)   A 8 7 4

    5 led   Q 9 3

This is a side suit in a trump contract. Declarer plays the ace from dummy. Do you play the nine or the three?

If West, as is probable, has led from the king he will know that you hold the queen, because if South had held this card he would have played low from dummy. It is therefore your duty, as East, to give partner a distributional signal, playing the lowest from three.

(2)   A K 7

    4 led   Q 8 3

West leads the four at notrumps and South plays the king from dummy. Now partner won't know about the queen; it is therefore right to encourage with the eight.

(3)   A K 5

    Q led   10 6 2

The queen is led at notrumps and the king is played from dummy. Now you should assume that partner has led from Q J 9 x or Q J 9 x x, and the most helpful card is the ten.

(4)   A 8 3

    K led   7 2

The king is led, presumably from K Q J or K Q 10, and declarer plays low from dummy. If the lead is from K Q 10 x x West will want to know whether it is safe to continue. The right card now is the seven—high-low from a doubleton. If you held the jack you would be playing it, so the seven will tell partner that South is trying a Bath coup (playing low from J x x).

[98]

These situations are not too difficult if you ask yourself the simple question. What does partner want to know?

One other signal is the so-called trump peter to indicate three cards in the trump suit. With 7 4 2 you play high-low to give partner the count. There are two ways of using this signal. Some players use the trump peter only when it is important for partner to know that there is a possibility of a ruff with the third trump. Others—the majority—use the signal consistently, to assist partner in counting the hand.

SUIT PREFERENCE SIGNAL

No doubt you have heard tell of suit preference signals. If you don't play them you are depriving yourself of an extremely valuable defensive aid.

The general idea is that when the card you play has no special value you should attempt to convey a message to partner. A very common situation arises on this deal:

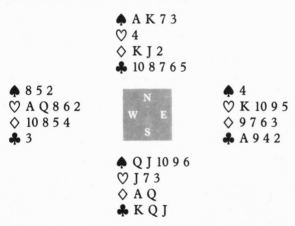

```
              ♠ A K 7 3
              ♡ 4
              ◇ K J 2
              ♣ 10 8 7 6 5
♠ 8 5 2                        ♠ 4
♡ A Q 8 6 2                    ♡ K 10 9 5
◇ 10 8 5 4                     ◇ 9 7 6 3
♣ 3                            ♣ A 9 4 2
              ♠ Q J 10 9 6
              ♡ J 7 3
              ◇ A Q
              ♣ K Q J
```

South is in four spades and West leads the three of clubs. East reads this for a singleton and after winning with the ace returns the *nine* of clubs, a high card to indicate that his only possible entry lies in the high suit, hearts, rather than in diamonds. West therefore ruffs and returns a low heart, thus neatly defeating the contract.

Once you get into the swing of using suit preference signals, you will find that they operate in many different situations. For example, when simply following suit with three low cards, such as 7 4 2, you may play them from the top to tell partner that your values lie in a particular side suit.

Suit preference signals apply only when cards cannot have their normal meaning of showing length or strength. This deal is an example of a defender's miscalculation:

♠ K 6
♡ Q 9 6 5 3
◇ 6 5 2
♣ A Q J

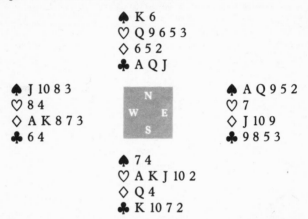

♠ J 10 8 3
♡ 8 4
◇ A K 8 7 3
♣ 6 4

♠ A Q 9 5 2
♡ 7
◇ J 10 9
♣ 9 8 5 3

♠ 7 4
♡ A K J 10 2
◇ Q 4
♣ K 10 7 2

West led the king of diamonds against four hearts and East, who had recently learned about suit preference signals, played the jack of diamonds, hoping that this would tell his partner to switch to a spade. What happened, of course, is that West read him for a doubleton diamond and led three rounds of the suit. Then a spade from dummy went away on the fourth club. If East had played the nine of diamonds on the opening lead it would have been perfectly easy for West to switch to a spade.

6

In dummy play

CAPTURING HONOURS

We look first at a few positions where shortage of entries forces the declarer to play a long suit from his own hand. This is a simple example:

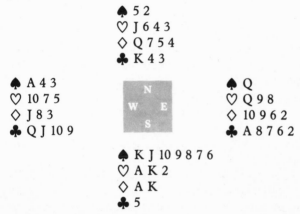

```
                    ♠ 5 2
                    ♡ J 6 4 3
                    ◇ Q 7 5 4
                    ♣ K 4 3
    ♠ A 4 3                       ♠ Q
    ♡ 10 7 5          N           ♡ Q 9 8
    ◇ J 8 3       W     E         ◇ 10 9 6 2
    ♣ Q J 10 9       S            ♣ A 8 7 6 2
                    ♠ K J 10 9 8 7 6
                    ♡ A K 2
                    ◇ A K
                    ♣ 5
```

Playing in four spades, South ruffs the second club and is forced to play trumps from his own hand. There is only one sensible play: lead the king and hope to drop a singleton queen. To lead a low card, hoping to find a singleton ace, is silly because you will still lose a second trick to an opponent who began with Q x x.

Suppose, next, that you were able to lead this suit from dummy and that second hand played low. Again, the best chance is to go up with the king, aiming to drop a singleton queen. It is true that a finesse of the jack might find West with A x, but this is only an even chance as compared with West holding Q x. If the suit is 3–1 South needs to drop a singleton queen, and this tilts the balance.

Some combinations are slightly deceptive:

5

A Q 10 9 6 2

You would like to establish this suit for the loss of just one trick. You lead the five from dummy and East plays low. Now the ten would be best if West held K x x, the queen if he held J x x. An even chance, then? No, West might hold J x. In this case a finesse of the queen will achieve your aim. Note that if West held K x you would lose two tricks however you played.

This holding is deceptive:

7

A J 10 6 4 2

Again you lead low from dummy and East plays low. If you need five tricks you must finesse, playing East for K Q x; but if you need only four tricks, ace followed by a low card is best, gaining when either opponent holds a doubleton K x or Q x.

This is a fairly frequent trump combination:

6 4 3
Q J 8 7 5 2

Assume that the declarer's only entry to dummy has already been removed. He leads the three of trumps and East follows with the nine or ten. There is not a lot in it, but on balance it is right for South to play low, gaining when West holds a singleton king or ace.

TACTICS IN FINESSING

When you propose to finesse in a suit where you hold several honours, always consider whether you can afford to lead a high card from the opposite hand.

9 6 4

K 8 7 3   Q

A J 10 5 2

To lead the nine would be a mistake, as you see. There are many combinations of this sort: for example, J x x opposite A K 10 x x. This is a common holding:

J 9 4

7 3   K 8 5 2

A Q 10 6

You can always win four tricks as the cards lie, but if you begin with the jack, and East plays low, you will need a further entry to dummy to pick up the suit. Here you should start with the nine from dummy. It is the same when you hold Q 9 x opposite A J 10 x.

This combination is elementary:

Q 6 3

10 8 2   K 9

A J 7 5 4

If you begin with the queen you can never take all five tricks, because East will cover. You must follow the general principle of leading low, winning five tricks when East holds K x.

The situation is tricky when the nine is added:

Q 6 3

A J 9 5 4

There are three ways in which you may aim to make all the tricks: finesse the jack and play the ace to drop East's K x; lead the queen and, if this is covered, take a subsequent finesse of the nine, playing East for K 10 x; lead the queen and, if this is covered, play to drop the ten on the next round. You may be relieved to hear that mathematically there is almost nothing to choose between the different lines. However, an interesting point arises when the distribution is (or might be):

Q 6 3

10 8 2   K 7

A J 9 5 4

Say that declarer begins by leading low to the jack. At this point many players in the West position would drop a misleading eight, seeking to persuade the declarer that he should cross to dummy and lead the queen. All one can say is that if you judge your opponent capable of this false card you must not be influenced. If West plays the two, however, there may be an inference that he holds just 10 2, not 10 8 2 or 10 7 2.

Another interesting position arises if you exchange the eight and the nine, as in this position:

Q 7 4 2

10 9 5   K 3

A J 8 6

Declarer begins by leading low to the jack. If West drops the five, then South's only chance for four tricks is to follow with the ace. West should therefore play the nine or ten. This is known as an obligatory false card, because it must be played to give the declarer an option. There are many positions of this sort, such as:

5

J 10 3   A 4

K Q 9 8 7 6 2

South leads the five to the queen. To give declarer a guess on the next round, West must drop the jack or ten.

NO FINESSE

There are many combinations where a finesse is playable but cannot help, assuming reasonable defence. Study this deal:

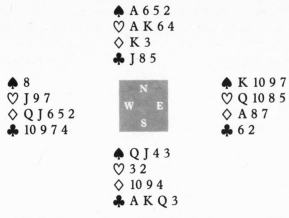

                    ♠ A 6 5 2
                    ♡ A K 6 4
                    ◇ K 3
                    ♣ J 8 5

♠ 8   ♠ K 10 9 7
♡ J 9 7   ♡ Q 10 8 5
◇ Q J 6 5 2   ◇ A 8 7
♣ 10 9 7 4   ♣ 6 2

                    ♠ Q J 4 3
                    ♡ 3 2
                    ◇ 10 9 4
                    ♣ A K Q 3

You play in four spades and West leads the queen of diamonds. The king is covered by the ace and East switches to a club. You must not be tempted now to run the queen of spades, a play that can scarcely gain. Instead, you must cross to the ace and return a spade. As the cards lie, this holds East to one trick.

This position is a little deceptive:

                    10 7 2

Q   K 9 8 6

            A J 5 4 3

If you need four tricks, your best chance is to lead low from dummy and finesse the jack, playing East for K x or Q x. But suppose three tricks will be enough; then the right play is ace from hand, gaining when West has a singleton queen or king.

The next combination is familiar but is often wrongly played:

                    J 7 4

                    A K 6 3

The best play for three tricks is to cash the ace, then lead low to the J 7. This line succeeds when West holds Q 10 x x. Playing off ace and king gains only when East holds Q x, which is less likely than two small. The result is the same with either play when West holds

Q x and East 10 x x x. The best play on a similar combination depends on the picture you have formed of the opposing hands.

A Q 6 3

J 7 4

Any play is good enough for three tricks when the division is 3–3. When the opposing cards are 4–2 you can save a trick only when there is a doubleton K x and you judge, or guess, which defender is likely to be short. If East has K x you lead low from dummy; if West, you must finesse the queen. (Technically, it does no harm to play off the ace first, but the chance of dropping a singleton king is so slight that the play is seldom advisable.)

DEEP FINESSES

There are numerous situations where the best play is a fairly deep finesse. Study this diagram:

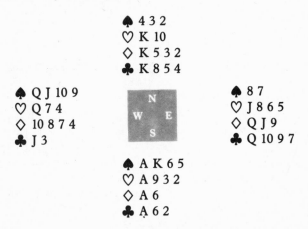

```
                    ♠ 4 3 2
                    ♡ K 10
                    ◇ K 5 3 2
                    ♣ K 8 5 4
  ♠ Q J 10 9                      ♠ 8 7
  ♡ Q 7 4          N              ♡ J 8 6 5
  ◇ 10 8 7 4    W     E           ◇ Q J 9
  ♣ J 3            S              ♣ Q 10 9 7
                    ♠ A K 6 5
                    ♡ A 9 3 2
                    ◇ A 6
                    ♣ A 6 2
```

You are in 3NT and West leads the queen of spades. As this suit does not present a great danger, and a switch to diamonds might not be welcome, you decide to win.

There are eight tricks on top and two chances—possibly three—for a ninth. A 3–3 break in clubs (or in spades, less likely)

[106]

would see you home. It is reasonable to try for this first, but slightly better to begin with a low heart to the ten. You duck the next round of spades, win the third round, and succeed eventually because you are able to develop a third trick in hearts. All you needed in this suit was to find West with a doubleton or trebleton honour.

There are many combinations where the first move should be a deep finesse. You are probably familiar with this one:

A Q 9

J 10 4 2   K 8 7

6 5 3

You cannot hope to make more than two tricks with the North-South cards. A finesse of the nine gives you an extra chance. It is three to one against finding West with both jack and ten, but you lose nothing, because you can finesse the queen on the next round.

A J 9

Q 10 4   K 8 7 2

6 5 3

This diagram presents a combination finesse with what film critics would call psychological overtones. As the cards lie, you could finesse the nine and so develop two tricks. However, an experienced defender in the West position might go up with the queen in front of dummy's A J 9. This would create a problem: you could play West for K Q x instead of Q 10 x. Between experts this sort of situation is a guessing game. Note that a defender can make the same kind of play with K 10 x in front of A J 9.

How would you play this next combination for four tricks?

A 9

K 10 6 4 2

It is right to finesse dummy's nine. You succeed when West has J x or Q x, as well as against all 3–3 divisions. This is a similar position:

A 10

K J 6 4 2

You can always make five tricks if the division is 3–3 and you find the queen. There is a slight advantage in finessing the ten on the first round, because then you succeed against West's Q x. You can never make five tricks when East has the doubleton.

ELIMINATION PLAY

In an earlier section we gave some examples of elimination play. It's a big subject, but in its simpler forms very easy to understand. As you surely know, it is generally easier to develop tricks in a suit when an opponent leads the suit than when you play it from your own hand. "Elimination play" means that you eliminate cards from an opponent's hand so that when he gains the lead he will be obliged to make the first (or the next) play in a critical suit.

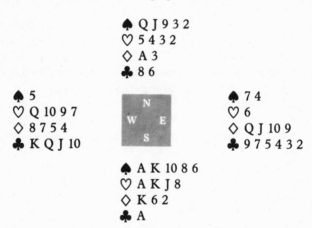

<pre>
              ♠ Q J 9 3 2
              ♡ 5 4 3 2
              ◇ A 3
              ♣ 8 6
  ♠ 5   ♠ 7 4
  ♡ Q 10 9 7   ♡ 6
  ◇ 8 7 5 4   ◇ Q J 10 9
  ♣ K Q J 10   ♣ 9 7 5 4 3 2
              ♠ A K 10 8 6
              ♡ A K J 8
              ◇ K 6 2
              ♣ A
</pre>

You play in six spades and West leads the king of clubs. Perhaps, at the table, you would draw trumps, cash the ace of hearts, cross to dummy and lead a second heart. East shows out. Unlucky, one down!

But you ought to have made this contract. After the ace of clubs draw two rounds of trumps, cross to the ace of diamonds, and *eliminate* clubs by ruffing the second round. Cash the ace of hearts. Play king of diamonds and ruff a diamond, *eliminating* this suit. The position is now:

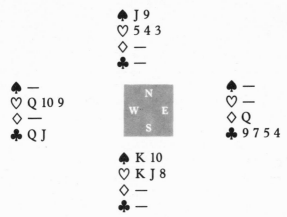

♠ J 9
♡ 5 4 3
◇ —
♣ —

♠ —
♡ Q 10 9
◇ —
♣ Q J

♠ —
♡ —
◇ Q
♣ 9 7 5 4

♠ K 10
♡ K J 8
◇ —
♣ —

The lead is in dummy and when you play a heart East shows out. No matter, you play low from hand. West wins but has no good return. Note, incidentally, that if the entry situation had been different and you had been forced to lead from your own hand at the finish, the play of the eight of hearts would have ensured the contract.

You will surely see now how to set about a hand of this type:

♠ A 7
♡ A J 5 3 2
◇ 10 8 5
♣ 4 3 2

♠ K 8 2
♡ K Q 10 9 8
◇ Q 4
♣ A Q 10

You are in four hearts and West, who has opened one diamond, begins with three rounds of this suit. You simply draw trumps, *eliminate* the spades by ruffing the third round, then play a club to the ten (or even the queen). When West takes this trick he will be forced to give you the contract even if he began with K J x of clubs.

If you reflect on it, you will agree that there are numerous combinations where you would prefer the opposition to make the first play. If you can force the player on your left to lead the suit, then such frail holdings as K x or A Q are proof against a losing finesse. As you well know from experience, you can be sure of a trick from Q x x opposite J x x if the opponents can be forced to lead the suit. There are innumerable situations of this kind and literally none where your chances are better if you have to lead the suit yourself.

WHEN THERE ARE TWO CHANCES

Much of the skill in this game lies in taking all the chances in the right order. How would you have managed the play on this deal?

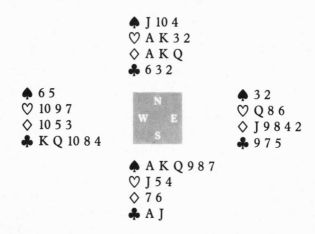

```
              ♠ J 10 4
              ♡ A K 3 2
              ◇ A K Q
              ♣ 6 3 2
♠ 6 5                         ♠ 3 2
♡ 10 9 7          N           ♡ Q 8 6
◇ 10 5 3      W     E         ◇ J 9 8 4 2
♣ K Q 10 8 4      S           ♣ 9 7 5
              ♠ A K Q 9 8 7
              ♡ J 5 4
              ◇ 7 6
              ♣ A J
```

You find yourself in seven spades and West leads the king of clubs. You win and draw trumps in two rounds. Now, perhaps, you hastily discard your losing club on the third round of diamonds, cash the ace of hearts, ruff a club, and play off all the spades. The opposition is not embarrassed and you finish one down.

[110]

You would have made this contract if the queen of hearts had dropped in two rounds, and there were faint chances for a squeeze, but you missed the best chance. You could have given yourself the chance of either the queen of hearts falling in two rounds, or of the suit breaking 3–3. After drawing trumps cash ace and king of hearts. When the queen does not appear, discard a *heart* on the third round of diamonds and ruff a heart. The suit breaks well and you can enter dummy with a third trump to discard your club loser on the thirteenth heart.

One of the present authors suffered as North on the following deal:

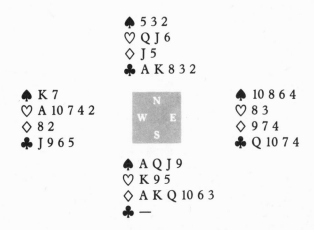

```
              ♠ 5 3 2
              ♡ Q J 6
              ◇ J 5
              ♣ A K 8 3 2
  ♠ K 7                        ♠ 10 8 6 4
  ♡ A 10 7 4 2                 ♡ 8 3
  ◇ 8 2                        ◇ 9 7 4
  ♣ J 9 6 5                    ♣ Q 10 7 4
              ♠ A Q J 9
              ♡ K 9 5
              ◇ A K Q 10 6 3
              ♣ —
```

South was in six diamonds and West began with ace and another heart. In with the king of hearts, South crossed to the jack of diamonds, ruffed a low club, and played off all the trumps. Then he crossed to the queen of hearts and discarded two spades on the ace and king of clubs. The spade finesse could not be avoided and West made his king.

The declarer was unconscious of error, but he lost his best chance for this contract on the opening lead. If he drops the king of hearts under the ace at trick one he has enough entries to play for a 4–4 break in clubs, which in theory is about a 33% chance. Win the second heart in dummy, ruff a club, ace and another diamond, ruff a club; now play off all the trumps, discarding two spades from dummy, cross to the queen of hearts, and you will find that the A K 8 of clubs are all good.

The extra chance on the following deal is perhaps easy to miss.

```
                    ♠ Q 10 6 4
                    ♡ 9 6 5 2
                    ◇ A K J
                    ♣ 9 4

    ♠ 7 3                           ♠ 5
    ♡ K Q 10 4          N           ♡ A J 8 3
    ◇ 10 8 2      W          E      ◇ Q 9 7 3
    ♣ A J 6 3          S           ♣ Q 7 5 2

                    ♠ A K J 9 8 2
                    ♡ 7
                    ◇ 6 5 4
                    ♣ K 10 8
```

Playing in four spades, South ruffs the second heart and draws trumps in two rounds. He sees two chances—the diamond finesse and the lie of the clubs. Unlucky, the jack of diamonds loses to the queen and the king of clubs is decapitated.

What do you think of the declarer's play? He could have done better in rather subtle fashion. The first move, after trumps have been drawn, should be a low club to the eight and jack. West exits with a diamond (or another heart). South now finesses the ten of clubs (which, as we explained on an earlier hand, is now a better than even chance). When the ten of clubs forces the ace, the king is established and the diamond finesse is not needed.

Suppose, next, that declarer's clubs had been simply 5 4 opposite K 10 3. It would still have been good play to begin with a club to the ten. This would gain when East held both queen and jack. If the ten loses to the queen or jack in West's hand, South can still take his two main chances—a club to the king and the diamond finesse.

PART III

Mistakes That May Be Forgiven

7

In bidding

THE RAISE TO GAME

Few types of player are more annoying than those who treat bidding as a conversation between partners and ignore tactical considerations. This happened to be the last deal of an important match and it proved costly for North-South.

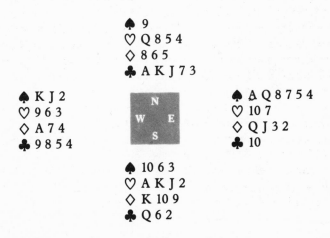

North-South were vulnerable and the bidding at one table went:

South	West	North	East
1♡	No	2♣	2♠
No	No	4♡	No
No	4♠	Dble	No
No	No		

Four spades was one down, but this was a very good result for East-West, obviously. At the other table North raised one heart to four hearts and East did not come in, since his hand was by no means without hope in defence. Ten tricks were made.

North, at the first table, was quite unabashed. "There might have been a slam our way", he said. "My hand was worth a delayed game raise."

If North-South had held the higher suit, spades, and North had held an additional value, such as the queen of diamonds, there would have been some justification for his manoeuvres. As it was, he showed a complete lack of tactical sense.

WHEN BLACKWOOD IS SILLY

Blackwood for aces is certainly useful at times, but there are two occasions where it should be avoided. These are when the Blackwood bidder has a void and when he has an unguarded doubleton (or longer suit) and may not be sure, even after a favourable response, whether this particular suit is covered. For example, East-West hold:

West	East
♠ A Q 10 8 5 2	♠ K J 7 4
♡ K Q 6	♡ A J 3
◇ Q 4	◇ 10 8 7
♣ A Q	♣ K 9 3

The bidding goes:

West	East
1♠	4♠
4NT	5◇
6♠	No

Diamond led; one down. "That was unlucky", says West. "I had 19 points, but there was duplication in both hearts and clubs."

So there was, but the weakness in diamonds could have been identified. Over four spades West should have made a cue bid of five clubs. East bids five hearts, denying the ace of diamonds. Now the partnership can stop in five spades.

This rather difficult hand trapped almost every pair in a duplicate game:

West	East
♠ A J 10 9 4	♠ 8 7 6 5 2
♡ —	♡ A Q
◇ K Q 10 4	◇ A 5 2
♣ A J 3 2	♣ 7 6 4

After one spade—four spades it was certainly tempting for West to go straight to slam. Unfortunately there was no way to avoid the loss of a trump and a club. The only pair to avoid the slam bid as follows:

West	East
1♠	4♠
5♣ (1)	5◇
5♡	5♠ (2)
No (3)	

(1) Holding a void, West prefers cue bids to Blackwood.

(2) Partner's five hearts is illuminating. If East's A Q is opposite a void, the hand is not impressive.

(3) West realizes that there may be duplication in hearts and that there are gaps in the black suits.

RESPONDING AT THE TWO LEVEL

One of the main differences between tournament players and rubber bridge players is seen in the first response to an opening bid of one. Take a hand of this sort:

```
        ♠ 7 5 3
        ♡ A Q 6 3 2
        ◇ Q 7
        ♣ K Q 8

        ♠ K 6 4
        ♡ 4
        ◇ J 8 6 3
        ♣ A J 5 4 2
```

North has a minimum, but nevertheless a sound, opening of one heart. At rubber bridge most South players would blithely respond two clubs. Now North has to say something and whether he chooses two hearts or (better) three clubs, the partnership will probably be overboard. Here South, with a bad fit and only nine points, should respond 1NT. North will pass and 1NT will be made.

Another common mistake is to overbid after an original pass. Observe this little tragedy:

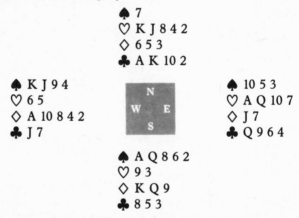

```
                    ♠ 7
                    ♡ K J 8 4 2
                    ◇ 6 5 3
                    ♣ A K 10 2

♠ K J 9 4                              ♠ 10 5 3
♡ 6 5                                  ♡ A Q 10 7
◇ A 10 8 4 2                           ◇ J 7
♣ J 7                                  ♣ Q 9 6 4

                    ♠ A Q 8 6 2
                    ♡ 9 3
                    ◇ K Q 9
                    ♣ 8 5 3
```

At game all the bidding followed this treacherous course:

South	West	North	East
No (1)	No	1♡ (2)	No
2♠ (3)	No	3♣ (4)	No
3NT	No	No	Dble
No	No	No	

(1) Many players would open, but we fully agree with the pass. Where are you going if partner cannot open in third hand?

(2) Again, many players would open in third position, but we see more danger than advantage in such a bid.

(3) "I wanted to show you I had almost an opening bid", said South afterwards.

(4) There was not much to choose at this point between 2NT and three clubs. North expected his partner to hold heart support.

West led a diamond against 3NT doubled and South made only five tricks. The worst bid was his jump to two spades. The time to jump, following a pass, is when you hold good support for partner and can expect a game opposite any sound opening. The hands were a poor fit, of course, and the opposing cards lay badly, but if South had responded one spade the partners could have played in 2NT, which would not have been doubled.

RESPONDING TO A TAKE-OUT DOUBLE

With both sides vulnerable, the bidding begins:

South	West	North	East
—	1♡	Dble	No
?			

South holds:

(1)   ♠ 6 5
        ♡ K J 9 6 3
        ◇ 10 8 4 2
        ♣ Q 3

What would you respond? There are three possibilities: pass, 1NT, two diamonds. One of these would be very bad. Which?

What you must not do is pass for penalties. You are sitting under the heart bidder and your K J 9 6 3 won't stop him making tricks with a fair suit.

As between 1NT and two diamonds, we prefer 1NT. You have a good holding in hearts and to play in two diamonds might be silly.

After the same bidding South holds:

(2)
♠ 6 5 2
♡ 10 8 6 3
◇ J 7 4
♣ 9 6 5

In this unpleasant situation there are four possible actions: pass, one spade, 1NT, two clubs.

It is certainly wrong to pass. One heart doubled, with two overtricks, would give the opponents 60 below, 50 for the insult, and 400 for the overtricks. Partner would not be at all pleased, especially if he had a good hand with length in spades.

What about one spade? Many players would make this call, claiming that it was the "cheapest" bid available. But it ceases to be cheap if partner raises to three or four spades, thinking that at least you will hold some sort of spade suit. To respond in a three-card major is permissible if you hold either a few points or a doubleton elsewhere, but it is idiotic on a very weak balanced hand.

So the choice is between 1NT and two clubs. We advise 1NT unless your partner has the old-fashioned idea that this response promises some values.

Still with the same sequence:

South	West	North	East
—	1♡	Dble	No
?			

South holds:

(3)
♠ 6 2
♡ Q J 9 8 6 4
◇ 5 4 3
♣ 7 2

Well, now you must pass for penalties, not so much because you expect 200 or more as because you really have no alternative. And what do you expect North to lead if the bidding stays in one heart doubled? Right, a trump, even if he has a singleton. The object of the defence here is to extract low trumps from the declarer.

A slightly different problem: after the same sequence South holds:

(4)   ♠ A 8 7 4
            ♡ 6 5 3
            ◇ K 10 5 3
            ♣ 4 2

Many players would jump to two spades, saying later "I had to show you I was better than minimum". But what is the point of this very debatable jump? If partner raises to three spades you won't like to pass and you won't be at all confident of making four spades. The folly of jumping to two spades can be seen if you consider what may happen over a simple response of one spade. Say that partner raises to two spades: your hand will barely be worth a raise to game, and with many partners three spades would be enough.

WHEN PARTNER OVERCALLS WITH 2NT

West opens one spade, North, your partner, overcalls with 2NT, and East passes. What do you understand by partner's 2NT? Initially, that he has length in both minors? Correct! This convention is popular in almost all classes of play.

But suppose the bid of 2NT occurs later in the auction, as in this sequence:

South	West	North	East
—	—	—	1♡
No	2♡	2NT	No
?			

Your hand is:

            ♠ Q J 9 2
            ♡ J 6 4
            ◇ 3 2
            ♣ 10 6 4 2

Now North, in theory, might hold a minor two-suiter or he might hold a stronger hand, no doubt with a good minor suit. The modern tendency is to treat all such bids as two-suiters.

It is worth adding that many players are altogether too fond of these 2NT bids. If the player on your right opens one heart and you hold

♠ 5 2
♡ 4
♢ K J 8 5 2
♣ A Q 7 4 3

it is absurd to come in with 2NT. Just wait and see which way things are going. By showing the nature of your hand you make it much easier for the opponents to judge how high to go and how to play if they win the contract.

If you have already passed, by the way, an overcall of 1NT is sufficient to indicate a shapely two-suiter. Say that the bidding begins:

South	West	North	East
No	1◇	No	1♡
1NT			

Here South is not saying "Although I passed originally, I have a fair balanced hand". That would be *very* amateurish. South should hold a strong spade-club two-suiter, something like:

♠ A J 8 7 3
♡ 5
♢ 4
♣ K J 9 6 4 2

The 1NT overcall may lead to a profitable sacrifice.

SIMPLE OVERCALLS

What standard do you apply when you are considering a simple overcall such as one spade over an opponent's one diamond, or two diamonds over one spade? If you put this question to an average player he may well reply: "Not so many points as for an opening bid, because it's only an overcall."

This reply shows little understanding. There are various possible motives for a defensive overcall and they have little to do with points. These are all possible reasons for an overcall:

1. You may prevent the opponents from bidding an easy 3NT. For example, if you have a good suit such as K Q J 9 x and not much else, they won't *know* that you have no side entry.

2. You may be indicating a good lead to your partner.

3. Just as important as either of these, many overcalls occupy *space*. If you can overcall one club with one spade you may well cause the opponents a small problem. Tournament players devote a great deal of thought to devising conventions to meet this problem.

4. Finally, of course, you may find partner with good values and be able to compete for the contract.

The *worst* overcalls are those at the level of two when the player has, relatively speaking, more in defence than in attack. This deal is an example:

```
              ♠ 10 7 6
              ♡ Q 9 8 5
              ◇ 8 7
              ♣ 9 7 5 3

♠ 8 2                          ♠ K Q J 9 3
♡ K 6 4 2         N            ♡ A J 10
◇ K J 9 5      W     E         ◇ 6 4
♣ A 8 2           S            ♣ Q J 10

              ♠ A 5 4
              ♡ 7 3
              ◇ A Q 10 3 2
              ♣ K 6 4
```

The bidding goes:

South	West	North	East
—	No	No	1♠
2◇	Dble	No	No
No			

West leads a spade and South ends with just three tricks, 900 down. "Did you see my hand?" he exclaims. "I had the best hand at the table, 14 points and a good suit." Well, nearly!

But after partner had passed, what did this overcall stand to gain? Admittedly, the cards were stacked against it, but if partner had held one or two useful cards, notably the jack of diamonds, there might have been no game for the opposition and two diamonds doubled would still have been expensive. Now look at a different sort of hand:

♠ 6 4
♡ A 8 3
♢ A J 10 9 8 3
♣ 5 2

Only nine points—for those who assess in this way—but a perfectly sound overcall, since the player can hardly fail to make five or six tricks even if partner is weak. It is better to hold few points and a good suit than the other way round.

WHEN PARTNER HAS DOUBLED AN OVERCALL

The bidding begins:

South	West	North	East
1♠	2♡	Dble	No
?			

When do you stand the double and when do you take it out? Let's look at a few examples. South holds:

(1)   ♠ K J 10 8 4
           ♡ 5
           ♢ A 8 6 2
           ♣ K J 4

To take out the double would be ridiculous. Partner's spade lead will suit you and you have defensive tricks in both minors.

(2)   ♠ Q 9 7 6 4 2
             ♡ 4
             ◇ A K J 3
             ♣ Q 2

This is more difficult. Partners are liable to begin with ace of spades from ace and another, and sometimes they hold long diamonds and your tricks in this suit fail to mature. It could be wrong, but we would be inclined to take out into two spades.

(3)   ♠ K Q 9 7 2
             ♡ —
             ◇ A J 8 6 2
             ♣ Q 6 3

Don't pass and employ the silly argument: "As I was void in hearts I thought you'd have a long string." There are two good reasons for removing the double: you are void in hearts and you have a long second suit. Remove to three diamonds, not to two spades.

(4)   ♠ A 10 8 6 2
             ♡ —
             ◇ K J 9 4
             ♣ A 10 8 4

The void in hearts is unattractive, but here we would pass, if only because there is no good alternative.

When partner has doubled two of a minor, you must be more ready to take out, because his double will not necessarily contain such solid defence as when he doubles two of a major.

What about a double at the range of one? This should always express good trumps and moderate values, so you should remove it only with a very unsuitable hand. The bidding goes:

South	West	North	East
1◇	1♡	Dble	No
?			

You hold:

♠ A J 7 4
♡ 3
◇ A Q 9 6 4 2
♣ K 5

Don't think of taking out the double into either one spade or two diamonds. Partner should have at least four solid defensive tricks and the prospects in one heart doubled are good.

WHEN TO REOPEN

We conclude this chapter with some remarks about one of the most critical and poorly comprehended areas of the game: "protection" when opponents have died in a part score.

Take, first, the situation where an opening bid has been passed round to fourth hand, a sequence such as:

South	West	North	East
—	1♡	No	No
?			

Most of the textbooks will tell you that you can reopen with quite a weak hand, bidding one of a suit with about eight points upwards, 1NT with about 11–14, and doubling with suitable shape from about 11 points upwards. Those standards are reasonable, but there is a good deal more to say.

First, if you have the weak type, you have to consider what are the chances that partner may have passed on a big hand. After the sequence above you hold:

(1)   ♠ K 10 8 6 2
        ♡ 5 4
        ◇ K J 5
        ♣ J 9 2

Now there are sound reasons for bidding one spade. You have a reasonable suit; your shortage in hearts suggests that partner may have made a trap pass; and since you hold the other major, there is

[124]

little danger that the opponents may discover a fit and outbid you.

The prospects are much less encouraging when you hold:

(2) ♠ 10 7 2
     ♡ J 8 5
     ◇ A Q 6 4 2
     ♣ Q 9

Now you can be less certain that partner has made a trap pass—and if he has, you will take 100 or more from one heart; it is possible that if you give opponents another chance they will find a fit in spades; you are under strength for double, 1NT, or two diamonds.

What about 1NT in fourth position, when the opening bid has been followed by two passes? The standard usually quoted is 11–14. That is about right over the major suits, but in a sequence such as

South	West	North	East
—	1♣	No	No
1NT			

South should be stronger, more like 13–15; with less he can bid one of a suit. Note that the requirements for this 1NT in the protective position are the same whether or not you play a strong opening 1NT, and vulnerability makes little difference. Also, it is not entirely necessary to have a stopper in the opponent's suit.

Finally, have you ever considered the distinction between the two sequences below?

(1) South	West	North	East
—	1◇	No	1♡
No	2♡	No	No
?			

South holds:

     ♠ A Q J 2
     ♡ 7 4
     ◇ 8 3 2
     ♣ K Q 6 5

The opponents have died early, *after discovering a fit*. This means that they must be limited. You can rely on partner holding some useful values and it is safe to compete with two spades. If you had only three spades, with the queen of diamonds instead of the queen of spades, you could reopen with a protective double.

What about this sequence however?

(2)	South	West	North	East
	—	1◇	No	1♡
	No	2◇	No	No
	?			

Would you reopen on the same values? It's dangerous! Here the opponents have not discovered a fit of any sort. East may quite possibly hold a 4-4-1-4 10 count. If so, and if you reopen, you will be walking into the lion's den.

Remember, then, this distinction: when opponents subside at a low level after discovering a fit, they must be limited; but when they have not found a fit and they drop early, they may hold about 23 points between them and be poised to punish any intervention.

8

In defence

AN IMAGINATIVE LEAD

Here is a small problem for West, the opening leader, who holds:

♠ 9 4
♡ K 7 6 5 4
◇ 8 6
♣ J 9 7 4

The bidding has been:

South	West	North	East
1NT	No	2♣	No
2♡	No	3NT	No
No	No		

The normal lead, a heart, is not very attractive after South has shown four hearts. A spade is possible, even though North may be presumed to hold four cards in this suit. A club is possible, too, though here it is worth noting that East did not double the response of two clubs, as he might have done if he had held good clubs. Well, at the table West chose the eight of diamonds, which turned out to be a rather clever trick, since the full hand was:

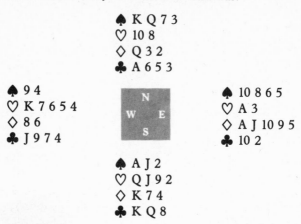

♠ K Q 7 3
♡ 10 8
♢ Q 3 2
♣ A 6 5 3

♠ 9 4
♡ K 7 6 5 4
♢ 8 6
♣ J 9 7 4

♠ 10 8 6 5
♡ A 3
♢ A J 10 9 5
♣ 10 2

♠ A J 2
♡ Q J 9 2
♢ K 7 4
♣ K Q 8

After the diamond lead had run to the king, South could cash only eight tricks before West came in again to lead another diamond.

West was a bit lucky, perhaps, since a club lead would certainly not have been a bad choice on his hand. Looking at the affair from the angle of North-South, one sees again that these Stayman responses are often very helpful to the opposition. With eleven points opposite a strong notrump, North could have gone straight to 3NT. Of course, South *might* have held something like J 10 x x in spades and A x x in hearts. Our opinion remains that Stayman responses on balanced hands are much overdone.

HOLD UP IN DEFENCE

Both West and East need to show good judgement if they are to defeat South's contract of four spades on this deal:

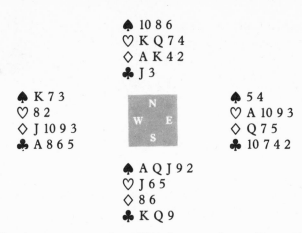

$\spadesuit$ 10 8 6
$\heartsuit$ K Q 7 4
$\diamondsuit$ A K 4 2
$\clubsuit$ J 3

$\spadesuit$ K 7 3
$\heartsuit$ 8 2
$\diamondsuit$ J 10 9 3
$\clubsuit$ A 8 6 5

$\spadesuit$ 5 4
$\heartsuit$ A 10 9 3
$\diamondsuit$ Q 7 5
$\clubsuit$ 10 7 4 2

$\spadesuit$ A Q J 9 2
$\heartsuit$ J 6 5
$\diamondsuit$ 8 6
$\clubsuit$ K Q 9

South opens one spade and North responds two diamonds, since a response of two hearts would suggest a five-card suit. South bids two spades and North raises to game.

West has a safe lead in diamonds, but this is unlikely to achieve anything. The doubleton heart is more purposeful, mainly because West holds a very likely trick in the trump suit.

When the eight of hearts is led, South plays the king from dummy, hoping to persuade a defender to part with the ace. East must consider whether his partner is more likely to hold a singleton or a doubleton, and also whether, in any case, it could help to play the ace and return a heart. This might, in some circumstances, be the best defence, but the odds are against it. In general, a defender should be more inclined to play his partner for a doubleton than a singleton.

East plays low, therefore, and South takes a spade finesse, losing to the king. West still needs to decide (ethically, without drawing an inference from partner's possible hesitation) that a second heart is the best defence.

Do not forget that all the standard moves in declarer's play—hold up, entry-killing and so forth—are equally available to the defending side.

Any player who is not at the beginner's stage will play high-low from a doubleton when his partner leads the king against a suit contract. It is just as important on many occasions to signify that you hold *four* cards. This is one such situation:

Q J 5

K 10 7 3   9 6 4 2

A 8

West leads the three against a notrump contract and the queen is played from dummy. East must not fail to play the six. Then, if West is first to gain the lead, he can continue the suit quite safely.

Signals to show length are extremely important when declarer plays towards a long suit in dummy, as here:

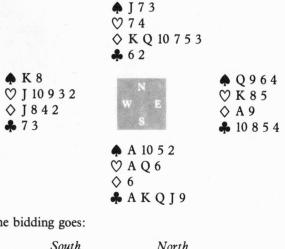

♠ J 7 3
♡ 7 4
◇ K Q 10 7 5 3
♣ 6 2

♠ K 8   ♠ Q 9 6 4
♡ J 10 9 3 2   ♡ K 8 5
◇ J 8 4 2   ◇ A 9
♣ 7 3   ♣ 10 8 5 4

♠ A 10 5 2
♡ A Q 6
◇ 6
♣ A K Q J 9

The bidding goes:

South	North
South	*North*
1♣	1◇
3NT	No

South's 3NT may not be classical, but we see nothing wrong with it.

West leads the jack of hearts and East correctly plays the eight, since he can be sure that his partner has led from J 10 9, not from A J 10. South wins and leads a low diamond to the queen. Unless West plays the eight on this trick, it is difficult for East to win with the ace, and clearly, if East holds up, South will run swiftly for home. The defence is simple if West plays the eight, because if this is from a doubleton East will never be able to shut out the suit.

It is extremely hard to play a good defence with a partner who does not afford these indications of length.

THE UPPERCUT

Many contracts can be defeated by judicious use of the play known as the "uppercut". This is a fairly simple example:

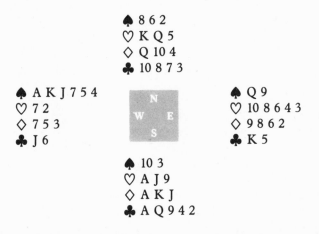

```
                    ♠ 8 6 2
                    ♡ K Q 5
                    ◇ Q 10 4
                    ♣ 10 8 7 3
♠ A K J 7 5 4                         ♠ Q 9
♡ 7 2              N                   ♡ 10 8 6 4 3
◇ 7 5 3         W     E                ◇ 9 8 6 2
♣ J 6              S                   ♣ K 5
                    ♠ 10 3
                    ♡ A J 9
                    ◇ A K J
                    ♣ A Q 9 4 2
```

South opens one club, West overcalls with one spade, and after a raise from his partner South finishes in five clubs. West begins with ace and king of spades. Now he can make the play a little easier for his partner by continuing with a low spade, forcing East to ruff high with K x or Q x of trumps; but even if West leads the jack of spades on the third round East must not fail to contribute the king of clubs, a card that can hardly cost the contract and may be essential.

[131]

The defence on the next deal requires a little more imagination on the part of the defenders:

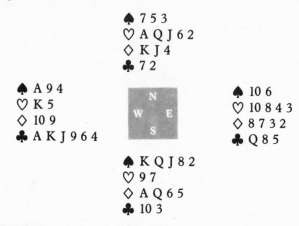

```
                    ♠ 7 5 3
                    ♡ A Q J 6 2
                    ◇ K J 4
                    ♣ 7 2
♠ A 9 4                              ♠ 10 6
♡ K 5                               ♡ 10 8 4 3
◇ 10 9                              ◇ 8 7 3 2
♣ A K J 9 6 4                       ♣ Q 8 5
                    ♠ K Q J 8 2
                    ♡ 9 7
                    ◇ A Q 6 5
                    ♣ 10 3
```

South plays in four spades and West begins with ace and king of clubs. As his partner has played the five and the eight, in that order, West knows that another club will concede a ruff-and-discard, often a fatal manoeuvre. However, on this occasion the only chance for the defence is to establish an extra trick in the trump suit. West must continue with a third club. Then he wins the first round of spades and leads a fourth club, on which his partner produces the ten of spades to ensure a happy ending for the defence.

UNBLOCKING BY THE DEFENCE

There are numerous situations where just a little thought by a defender will convince him of the necessity to unblock a high card. This is one example:

A 10 7 4 2

Q 5

Playing in notrumps, South leads the king of this suit at a point where West would prefer his partner to gain the lead. Obviously West must drop the queen, hoping that his partner will turn up with J x x. If West does not unblock, South will let the queen hold the next trick.

This is another combination of the same sort:

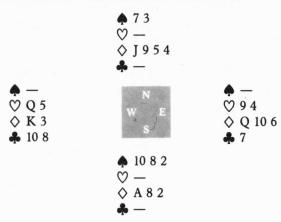

Spades are trumps and in this end-game South leads a diamond to the ace—or plays the ace from hand. West, if his side needs two more tricks, must not fail to drop the king, since otherwise he will be left on play after the next round of diamonds. The unblock would be necessary, too, if West held Q x and his partner K 10 x.

Such positions often arise in notrump contracts, as on this deal:

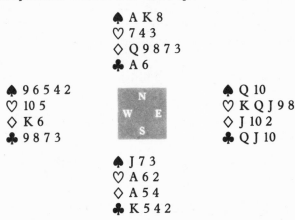

South plays in 3NT after East has overcalled in hearts. West leads the ten of hearts and South wins the second round. Probably his best line now is to cross to dummy and lead the seven of diamonds. If East plays low—perhaps from K x—declarer will duck and so prevent East from gaining the lead. As the cards lie, East will play the diamond jack and declarer the ace. It shouldn't be difficult now for West to unblock the king.

Suppose, next, that South leads the ace of diamonds from hand. Now West should think to himself, "If South had held something like A J x he would surely have crossed to dummy and finessed the jack." So again it is not difficult for West to play the king under the ace.

Do you think there is any way in which South can make his contract against any defence? It wouldn't be natural play, but a low diamond from hand wins the money. West must play low, the queen wins, and on the next round South plays low from hand, forcing West to take the king.

DUCKING IN DEFENCE

As we remarked earlier, the numerous machinations in declarer's play are all equally available to the defenders. The popular ducking play is an example.

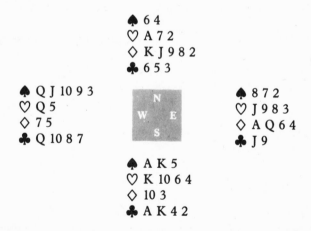

```
                    ♠ 6 4
                    ♡ A 7 2
                    ◇ K J 9 8 2
                    ♣ 6 5 3
♠ Q J 10 9 3                        ♠ 8 7 2
♡ Q 5              N                ♡ J 9 8 3
◇ 7 5          W       E            ◇ A Q 6 4
♣ Q 10 8 7            S             ♣ J 9
                    ♠ A K 5
                    ♡ K 10 6 4
                    ◇ 10 3
                    ♣ A K 4 2
```

Playing in 3NT, South wins the second spade and leads a slightly

[134]

cunning three of diamonds to dummy's jack. East must not be so foolish as to win and clear the spades. There is only one entry to dummy outside the diamonds and East's first objective must be to shut out the diamond suit by ducking the first round.

The situation on the next deal is similar, but here there is an interesting possibility for the declarer as well.

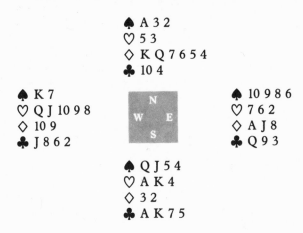

```
              ♠ A 3 2
              ♡ 5 3
              ◇ K Q 7 6 5 4
              ♣ 10 4
♠ K 7                         ♠ 10 9 8 6
♡ Q J 10 9 8     N            ♡ 7 6 2
◇ 10 9        W     E         ◇ A J 8
♣ J 8 6 2        S            ♣ Q 9 3
              ♠ Q J 5 4
              ♡ A K 4
              ◇ 3 2
              ♣ A K 7 5
```

In 3NT once again, South wins the second heart and leads a diamond to the queen. East has much the same problem as on the preceding deal: he must play low and so shut out dummy's suit.

Does anything else strike you? Do you think the declarer might have done better? He can, if he has reason to believe that East, not West, holds the ace of diamonds. Simply duck the first round, playing low from dummy! East wins and will probably try the ten of spades, hoping to force out dummy's entry. The queen is covered by the king; South plays low from dummy and thereafter loses only to the ace of diamonds.

HOLD UP IN THE TRUMP SUIT

There are some interesting positions where it is necessary for a defender to hold up a controlling card in the trump suit. This hand is not difficult:

[135]

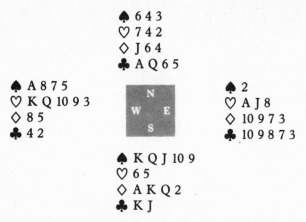

```
              ♠ 6 4 3
              ♡ 7 4 2
              ◇ J 6 4
              ♣ A Q 6 5
♠ A 8 7 5                      ♠ 2
♡ K Q 10 9 3      N           ♡ A J 8
◇ 8 5         W       E       ◇ 10 9 7 3
♣ 4 2             S           ♣ 10 9 8 7 3
              ♠ K Q J 10 9
              ♡ 6 5
              ◇ A K Q 2
              ♣ K J
```

Playing in four spades, South ruffs the third round of hearts and leads the king of spades. This is allowed to hold and he follows with the jack. West must duck again and now the contract cannot be made. If South plays another round of trumps he will go two down; the best he can do is play winners in the minor suits, allowing West to make his low trump. You see, of course, that if West wins the first or second round of trumps, then dummy will take care of a heart continuation.

A much more tricky situation arises on this deal:

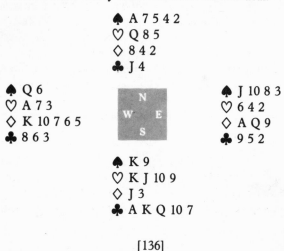

```
              ♠ A 7 5 4 2
              ♡ Q 8 5
              ◇ 8 4 2
              ♣ J 4
♠ Q 6                          ♠ J 10 8 3
♡ A 7 3           N           ♡ 6 4 2
◇ K 10 7 6 5  W       E       ◇ A Q 9
♣ 8 6 3           S           ♣ 9 5 2
              ♠ K 9
              ♡ K J 10 9
              ◇ J 3
              ♣ A K Q 10 7
```

The bidding goes:

South	North
1♣	1♠
2♡	3♡
4♡	No

North knows that his partner may hold only four hearts, but to raise hearts is the only sensible action.

The defence begins with three rounds of diamonds and South, with three top losers, is obliged to ruff. On the jack of hearts West plays low and East drops the six, beginning a high-low signal to indicate that he has three trumps. South follows with the king of hearts, but West is smart—he plays low again. This leaves:

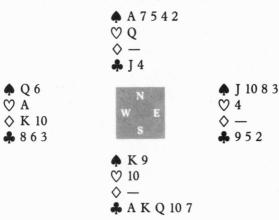

```
              ♠ A 7 5 4 2
              ♡ Q
              ◇ —
              ♣ J 4

♠ Q 6              N              ♠ J 10 8 3
♡ A           W       E          ♡ 4
◇ K 10            S              ◇ —
♣ 8 6 3                          ♣ 9 5 2

              ♠ K 9
              ♡ 10
              ◇ —
              ♣ A K Q 10 7
```

Whatever line South follows now, he is bound to lose two more tricks.

WHEN NOT TO OVERRUFF

When you have a chance to overruff the declarer (or the dummy), think again; and if any doubt remains, think a third time! Why it is often wrong to overruff appears in its simplest form when the cards lie like this:

6 3

K 10 5   7 4

A Q J 9 8 2

If at some point in the play South ruffs with the queen of trumps, obviously West can gain a trick by declining to overruff. The situation is often not so clear to a defender, but the general principle is sound: if your hand contains a probable trick in the trump suit, do not, as a rule, overruff.

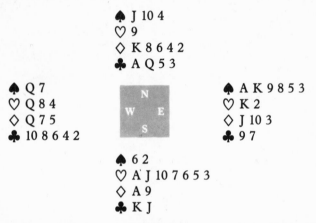

```
                    ♠ J 10 4
                    ♡ 9
                    ◇ K 8 6 4 2
                    ♣ A Q 5 3
    ♠ Q 7                              ♠ A K 9 8 5 3
    ♡ Q 8 4           N                ♡ K 2
    ◇ Q 7 5       W       E            ◇ J 10 3
    ♣ 10 8 6 4 2      S                ♣ 9 7
                    ♠ 6 2
                    ♡ A J 10 7 6 5 3
                    ◇ A 9
                    ♣ K J
```

South is in four hearts and West begins with queen and another spade. When East follows with a third spade South ruffs with the jack of hearts. West, who has a certain trump trick anyway, must not overruff. If he does, then South will pick up the remaining trumps with a simple finesse; but if West looks the other way and discards, East will later cover the nine of hearts with the king and West will make two trump tricks.

Refusal to overruff will sometimes produce an extra trick for quite a moderate trump holding. Say that the trumps lie like this:

5 2

10 7 6 3   Q J

A K 9 8 4

[138]

At an early stage of the play South ruffs with the nine. By declining to overruff West creates a second trick for his side.

In the same way a defender who holds good trumps must not be too quick to overruff the dummy.

Q

8 5   K 10 7 4

A J 9 6 3 2

South leads a side suit and ruffs with dummy's queen. If East overruffs, his side will make just two tricks in the trump suit; but if he declines to overruff, he stands to make three tricks.

BACKWARD FINESSES BY THE DEFENCE

There are some suit combinations where the defenders, with a view of the dummy, can play more accurately than the declarer might do with the same cards. This is true, especially, of backward finesses.

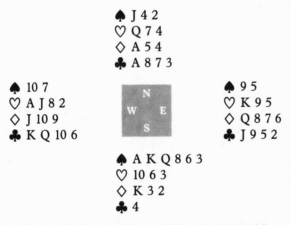

♠ J 4 2
♡ Q 7 4
◇ A 5 4
♣ A 8 7 3

♠ 10 7   ♠ 9 5
♡ A J 8 2   ♡ K 9 5
◇ J 10 9   ◇ Q 8 7 6
♣ K Q 10 6   ♣ J 9 5 2

♠ A K Q 8 6 3
♡ 10 6 3
◇ K 3 2
♣ 4

South plays in four spades and West leads the king of clubs. There may be an advantage in eliminating the clubs, so South begins with a club ruff, two rounds of spades, a club ruff, a diamond to the ace and a ruff of the last club. This leaves:

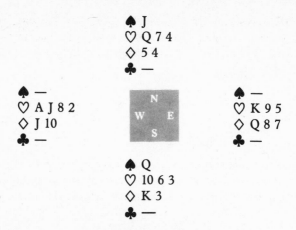

```
              ♠ J
              ♡ Q 7 4
              ◇ 5 4
              ♣ —
♠ —                           ♠ —
♡ A J 8 2                     ♡ K 9 5
◇ J 10                        ◇ Q 8 7
♣ —                           ♣ —
              ♠ Q
              ♡ 10 6 3
              ◇ K 3
              ♣ —
```

South exits with king and another diamond. It is evident that
West now must lead the jack of hearts, not a low one. If the declarer
had held this position in hearts he would probably have taken a
normal finesse, losing to the queen.

This is a similar position:

$$9 6 2$$

Q 7 5   K 10 8 3

$$A J 4$$

If East is on lead, the most effective card is the ten. This enables
the defence to establish quick winners. Note that here, too, a
declarer in the East or West position would normally lose two
tricks, taking a simple finesse of the ten and losing to the jack.

This is one more situation where the defenders may outguess the
declarer:

$$K 7 4$$

A Q 9 3   J 8 5

$$10 6 2$$

If West proposes to lead this suit, the best card is the queen.

Declarer will probably let this hold. West then follows with a low card and South has a guess, because West might have held Q J x x.

SECOND HAND HIGH

We end this chapter with two examples where second hand, despite the traditional injunction "second hand low, third hand high", must play a high card to embarrass the declarer. Here South is in 6NT and West leads the ten of spades.

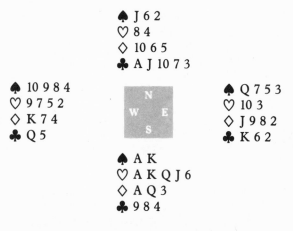

```
                    ♠ J 6 2
                    ♡ 8 4
                    ◇ 10 6 5
                    ♣ A J 10 7 3
  ♠ 10 9 8 4                        ♠ Q 7 5 3
  ♡ 9 7 5 2          N              ♡ 10 3
  ◇ K 7 4        W       E          ◇ J 9 8 2
  ♣ Q 5              S              ♣ K 6 2
                    ♠ A K
                    ♡ A K Q J 6
                    ◇ A Q 3
                    ♣ 9 8 4
```

South wins the spade lead and at an early stage leads the eight of clubs. It is easy to see that if West plays low South will duck in dummy and eventually make four tricks in clubs, enough for his contract. West must play the queen of clubs. Then, if the ace is played from dummy, East will hold off the next club and the contract will still be defeated.

A high club from West in this position would also be right if he held K x or Q x x or K x x. From South's angle, the queen or king might be from K Q x, so he might duck and finesse on the next round.

This defensive position is less well known:

```
                    ♠ 6 3
                    ♡ K 7 5
                    ◇ 4 2
                    ♣ A K 10 6 5 3
  ♠ Q 9 7                              ♠ A 8 4
  ♡ 9 4            ┌─────────┐         ♡ A J 10 8 3
  ◇ 10 8 7 6 5 3   │    N    │         ◇ Q 9
  ♣ J 2           W│       E │         ♣ Q 8 7
                   │    S    │
                   └─────────┘
                    ♠ K J 10 5 2
                    ♡ Q 6 2
                    ◇ A K J
                    ♣ 9 4
```

The bidding goes:

South	West	North	East
—	—	—	1♡
1♠	No	2♣	No
2NT	No	3NT	No
No	No		

West's lead of the nine of hearts runs to the declarer's queen.
South leads the four of clubs—and West must insert the jack! The
declarer must now cover with the king or go down at once, and
thereafter he has little chance to arrive at nine tricks. Note that the
same defence would be required if West held Q x of clubs instead of
J x.

9

In dummy play

TWENTY QUESTIONS

In this final chapter we are adopting a somewhat different style of presentation. Instead of describing at once how a hand should be played or defended, we exhort the reader to make the first attempt and follow with the answer. The hands are in no particular order; the common feature is that all represent situations that occur frequently. See how many questions you can answer correctly.

1.
　　　　　　　　　　♠ 4 3 2
　　　　　　　　　　♡ 8 7 5
　　　　　　　　　　◇ A 3 2
　　　　　　　　　　♣ J 7 5 3

♡6 led

　　　　　　　　　　♠ A K Q J 10 7
　　　　　　　　　　♡ J 3
　　　　　　　　　　◇ K 10 5 4
　　　　　　　　　　♣ A

You play in four spades and the defence begins with three rounds of hearts. You ruff and draw trumps in three rounds, East discarding a heart and a club. What next?

Answer: It is just a question of how you tackle the diamonds. If they break 3–3 there is no problem. If West has four to the queen or four to the jack you will lose two tricks unless the defence makes a mistake. The critical situation occurs when East has four diamonds, the suit being divided as follows:

A 3 2

J 9   Q 8 7 6

K 10 5 4

To play a diamond to the ace and finesse the ten on the way back doesn't help. The winning line is king first, low to the ace, and a third diamond from dummy, establishing a trick for the ten.

2.   ♠ 8 6
                              ♡ 7 3
                              ♢ A K Q J 3
                              ♣ J 9 7 4

♡K led

                        ♠ A K 7 4 3 2
                        ♡ 8 5 4
                        ♢ 10 9 2
                        ♣ A

The bidding goes:

South	North
—	1♢
1♠	2♢
3♠	4♠
No	

West leads the king of hearts, which holds the trick, and follows with a low spade, on which East plays the queen. How do you plan the play?

Answer: The defence has played well and the danger is that you may lose three hearts and a spade. One possibility is to cash ace and king of spades, then play on diamonds, hoping that the player who holds the outstanding trump will have to follow to three rounds; this will allow you to dispose of a heart on the fourth diamond.

There is a better line, however. Just refuse to win the first round of spades. Then, assuming the trumps are 3–2, there is nothing the opponents can do.

[144]

3.
      ♠ A K 2
      ♡ Q 10 8
      ◇ 4 2
      ♣ A K 5 3 2

♣ Q led

      ♠ 8 6 4 3
      ♡ —
      ◇ A K Q J 10 7 3
      ♣ 6 4

The bidding goes:

South	North
1◇	3♣
3◇	3NT
4◇	5◇
No	

Many players, it is true, would open with a pre-emptive four diamonds. It would certainly not be wrong to finish in six diamonds. All the more reason to make sure you don't go down in five!

West leads the queen of clubs. You play the king and lead a trump from dummy. "Wait a moment", says East. "It's not your lead". East, the wretch, has ruffed the first trick and now leads a diamond. The spades break 4–2, of course, and you finish an undignified one down. What has gone wrong?

Answer: Well, it was a mistake—a very slight mistake, but a mistake nevertheless—to play the king of clubs on the opening lead. You could have ducked twice and subsequently discarded two spades on the ace and king of clubs.

This form of play occurs more often when you hold something like A x x x x of a suit in dummy and one or two low cards in your own hand. When West leads the king it may be dangerous to play the ace from dummy, because if this is ruffed you will have lost a sure trick. It may be better, assuming you have losers elsewhere, to play low and keep the ace for a better day.

4.
♠ A 10 7 4 3
♡ 6
♢ J 10 2
♣ K 8 4 3

♠ K led

♠ —
♡ A K 9 8 7 5 4 3
♢ A K 6 4
♣ A

A difficult hand to bid; South opens two clubs and the bidding might continue:

South	North
2♣	2♠
3♡	3NT
6♡	No

West leads the king of spades. How do you plan the play?

Answer: There is no danger that the spade lead will be ruffed—West can hardly hold eight spades—but it is still right to play low, for a reason that is not too easy to see at first. Study the full hand:

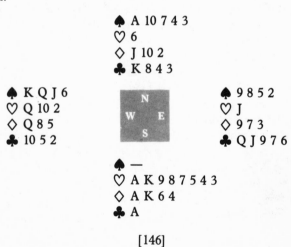

♠ A 10 7 4 3
♡ 6
♢ J 10 2
♣ K 8 4 3

♠ K Q J 6
♡ Q 10 2
♢ Q 8 5
♣ 10 5 2

♠ 9 8 5 2
♡ J
♢ 9 7 3
♣ Q J 9 7 6

♠ —
♡ A K 9 8 7 5 4 3
♢ A K 6 4
♣ A

If you win with the ace of spades you will have to take a diamond finesse at trick two and will lose eventually one diamond and one heart. It is better to ruff the opening lead and draw two rounds of trumps. Then you cash ace of clubs and exit with a heart. West wins this trick but has no good lead, for now there are two black winners in the dummy.

5.
      ♠ K J 5
      ♡ K J 8 3
      ◇ 5 4
      ♣ K Q 10 2

◇Q led

      ♠ A 9 6 3
      ♡ Q 10 7
      ◇ A K 2
      ♣ J 9 5

South opens a weak notrump and North raises to 3NT, spurning a Stayman response. West leads the queen of diamonds, on which East plays the six. How do you plan the play?

Answer: You have enough tricks for 3NT, provided always that you have time to develop them. The danger is that if you begin with the wrong suit the diamonds may be cleared and the hand with the long diamonds may hold an entry. For example, the hand may be:

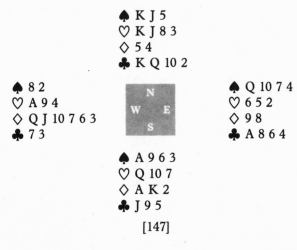

      ♠ K J 5
      ♡ K J 8 3
      ◇ 5 4
      ♣ K Q 10 2

♠ 8 2   ♠ Q 10 7 4
♡ A 9 4   ♡ 6 5 2
◇ Q J 10 7 6 3   ◇ 9 8
♣ 7 3   ♣ A 8 6 4

      ♠ A 9 6 3
      ♡ Q 10 7
      ◇ A K 2
      ♣ J 9 5

Suppose you win the first diamond and lead the nine of clubs to dummy's queen. East will win and return a diamond. Now you can take only eight tricks.

The hand shows that it is often right to hold up even when you hold two controls in the suit led. Suppose you win the second round of diamonds and lead a club: East wins but has no diamond to play, so the contract becomes easy.

Mind you, it is often right to take the first trick when you hold two controls in the suit that has been led. The deciding factors are: Would a switch to another suit be more dangerous—and might they find the switch? And can the dangerous opponent be kept out of the lead? Here it is just a guess who holds which ace, so the hold-up is surely correct.

6.
       ♠ 6 4 3
       ♡ Q 6
       ◇ 8 7 3
       ♣ 10 9 8 3 2

♡A led

       ♠ A K Q J 2
       ♡ 7
       ◇ A K J 10 4
       ♣ A Q

You have high hopes when you pick up your cards, but your partner shows no enthusiasm and you finish in four spades. West leads the ace of hearts and follows with the king. How do you play?

Answer: It is disappointing not to arrive at a slam on the South hand, but at least make sure you don't go down in game.

The danger here is that the whole hand may be:

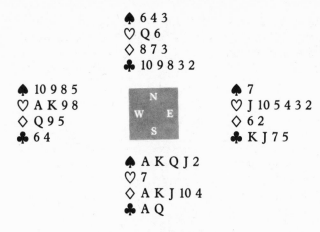

```
              ♠ 6 4 3
              ♡ Q 6
              ◇ 8 7 3
              ♣ 10 9 8 3 2

♠ 10 9 8 5                    ♠ 7
♡ A K 9 8                     ♡ J 10 5 4 3 2
◇ Q 9 5                       ◇ 6 2
♣ 6 4                         ♣ K J 7 5

              ♠ A K Q J 2
              ♡ 7
              ◇ A K J 10 4
              ♣ A Q
```

Suppose that you ruff the second heart and draw four rounds of trumps. When the queen of diamonds does not fall, you will end with nine tricks at most.

The safe play is to discard the queen of clubs on the second heart. Then your hand cannot be forced and you will lose just two hearts and a diamond.

7.

```
              ♠ Q 10 7 3 2
              ♡ 6 4
              ◇ 8 5 3
              ♣ A Q 5
```

♡K led

```
              ♠ A K 5 4
              ♡ 8 7 3
              ◇ A K J
              ♣ K J 10
```

You play in four spades. West's lead of the king of hearts is overtaken by the ace, and East returns the ten. West overtakes and plays a third heart. What will you do now?

Answer: Did you think of ruffing with the ten of spades, or the queen of spades, or a low spade? Any of these would be wrong. The theme is the same as on the previous deal. If you ruff you may establish a trump trick for the opposition and lose a diamond as well, the full hand being:

```
                    ♠ Q 10 7 3 2
                    ♡ 6 4
                    ◇ 8 5 3
                    ♣ A Q 5
    ♠ 6                              ♠ J 9 8
    ♡ K Q J 9 5 2        N          ♡ A 10
    ◇ Q 9 4           W     E       ◇ 10 7 6 2
    ♣ 8 7 3              S          ♣ 9 6 4 2
                    ♠ A K 5 4
                    ♡ 8 7 3
                    ◇ A K J
                    ♣ K J 10
```

Simply discard a loser from dummy on the third heart (or, if you want to be jokey, the ace of clubs).

Could this play ever be wrong, do you think? Only if East held *four* spades and the diamond finesse would have been right.

8.
```
                    ♠ A 7 3
                    ♡ J 8 5
                    ◇ 6 3 2
                    ♣ A Q 10 4
```

♠K led

```
                    ♠ 10 6
                    ♡ A Q 10 9 7 2
                    ◇ K 10
                    ♣ K 8 2
```

West leads the king of spades against four hearts. How do you plan the play?

Answer: The test comes on the first trick. It would be poor play to win with the ace of spades in dummy, because the full hand might be:

♠ A 7 3
♡ J 8 5
♢ 6 3 2
♣ A Q 10 4

♠ K Q 8 4
♡ K 6
♢ A 7 4
♣ 9 6 5 3

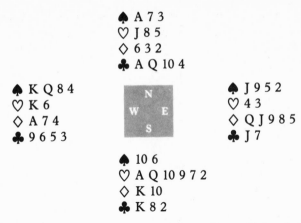

♠ J 9 5 2
♡ 4 3
♢ Q J 9 8 5
♣ J 7

♠ 10 6
♡ A Q 10 9 7 2
♢ K 10
♣ K 8 2

If you play the ace of spades at trick one, East will signal with the nine. When West comes in with the king of hearts he will put his partner in with the jack of spades and a return of the queen of diamonds will establish four tricks for the defence.

Taking the ace of spades at trick one is wrong in principle because it improves the communications of the defending side. So long as East can be kept out of the lead, South has a good chance to obtain a critical discard on the fourth round of clubs.

9.

♠ 8 2
♡ A 7 4
♢ K J 7 3 2
♣ A 6 4

♠6 led

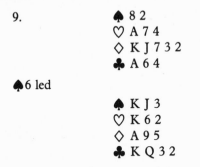

♠ K J 3
♡ K 6 2
♢ A 9 5
♣ K Q 3 2

You are in 3NT. West leads the six of spades, East plays the ten and you win with the jack. How do you plan the play?

Answer: It looks as though West has led from five or six spades headed by the A Q. You must take all precautions to avoid letting East gain the lead. The play is not difficult: cross to the ace of clubs and lead a low diamond from dummy, intending to insert the nine if East plays low. The hand may be:

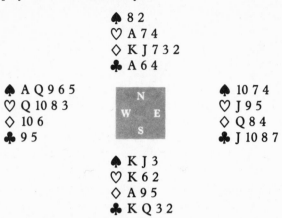

          ♠ 8 2
          ♡ A 7 4
          ◇ K J 7 3 2
          ♣ A 6 4

♠ A Q 9 6 5   ♠ 10 7 4
♡ Q 10 8 3   ♡ J 9 5
◇ 10 6   ◇ Q 8 4
♣ 9 5   ♣ J 10 8 7

          ♠ K J 3
          ♡ K 6 2
          ◇ A 9 5
          ♣ K Q 3 2

Suppose, next, that East were able to insert the ten of diamonds on the first round. The best play then would be to take ace and king of diamonds and follow with three rounds of clubs. Four tricks in clubs would be enough, and there might be other chances. For example, you might find West with four clubs. The play then would be to cash two hearts and give West the lead on the fourth round of clubs, playing him for 5–2–2–4 distribution.

10.

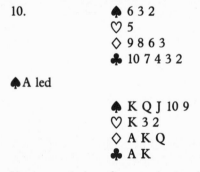

          ♠ 6 3 2
          ♡ 5
          ◇ 9 8 6 3
          ♣ 10 7 4 3 2

♠ A led

          ♠ K Q J 10 9
          ♡ K 3 2
          ◇ A K Q
          ♣ A K

You struggle into four spades by this route:

South	North
2♣	2◇
2♠	3♠
4♣	4♠
No	

It would not be wrong for North, over two spades, to bid 2NT, intending to support spades on the next round.

West begins with ace and another spade. How do you plan the play?

Answer: West has made a good lead, because you need at least one ruff and the defence may be able to extract dummy's third trump. The best play is the *king* of hearts; you hope that the player who holds the ace of hearts will not possess the outstanding trump.

The same kind of play would be right if your hearts were Q x x. West, perhaps holding A x of spades and ace of hearts, might be nervous of playing low, because you might have led the queen of hearts from a combination headed by K Q. True, the ace would be poor play on West's part, because he should realize that there was little chance to find his partner with one of the minor suit aces.

11.
```
          ♠ Q 6 5
          ♡ 8 4 2
          ◇ 9 6 5
          ♣ Q J 10 4
```

♠4 led

```
          ♠ A 10 2
          ♡ K Q J 10
          ◇ A J 4 3
          ♣ A K
```

You are in 3NT and West leads the four of spades. You play low from dummy and East contributes the nine. How do you plan the play?

Answer: Did you by any chance win with the ten of spades and then look round? Oh dear, back to the drawing-board!

```
                    ♠ Q 6 5
                    ♡ 8 4 2
                    ◇ 9 6 5
                    ♣ Q J 10 4
♠ K J 8 4 3                          ♠ 9 7
♡ 6 5              N                  ♡ A 9 7 3
◇ K 8 7        W       E              ◇ Q 10 2
♣ 6 3 2            S                  ♣ 9 8 7 5
                    ♠ A 10 2
                    ♡ K Q J 10
                    ◇ A J 4 3
                    ♣ A K
```

It is clear that if you take the first trick with the ten of spades and
lead the king of hearts, East will win and return his second spade.
This will surely hold you to eight tricks.

You must assume that West holds the king of spades and must
unblock the ace on the opening lead. Then you cash ace and king of
clubs and follow with the king of hearts. No problem now.

12.   ♠ K 7 5
                    ♡ A 6 3
                    ◇ A 6 5 2
                    ♣ 9 7 4

♡K led

                    ♠ A Q J 10 9 8
                    ♡ 7 2
                    ◇ Q 3
                    ♣ A 8 3

Over South's one spade North is hardly worth a raise to three
spades. He may bid two diamonds, then raise two spades to three,
which is not quite so encouraging a sequence. South bids the game
and West leads the king of hearts. How do you plan the play?

Answer: It would be a mistake to duck the first heart, if only
because a switch to clubs would be awkward. Having won with the
ace of hearts, did you play a round of trumps? Wrong on this
occasion, because there is a block in the spade suit and you need all

[154]

dummy's entries to make anything of the queen of diamonds. Suppose the full hand to be:

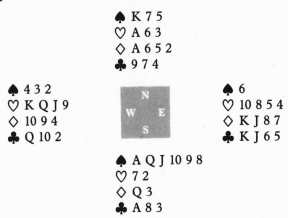

                    ♠ K 7 5
                    ♡ A 6 3
                    ◇ A 6 5 2
                    ♣ 9 7 4

♠ 4 3 2   ♠ 6
♡ K Q J 9   ♡ 10 8 5 4
◇ 10 9 4   ◇ K J 8 7
♣ Q 10 2   ♣ K J 6 5

                    ♠ A Q J 10 9 8
                    ♡ 7 2
                    ◇ Q 3
                    ♣ A 8 3

Win with the ace of hearts and lead a low diamond from dummy. East will probably win with the king and return a low heart, showing that he held four originally. The defenders may switch to clubs now, but you can win with the ace, cash queen of diamonds, and enter dummy on the third round of spades to discard a club on the ace of diamonds.

13.   ♠ A K 2
                    ♡ 8 6 3
                    ◇ A K 6 3 2
                    ♣ 9 4

♡Q led

                    ♠ Q J 10 7 4 3
                    ♡ A 7 4
                    ◇ 8 5
                    ♣ A K

The bidding might go:

South	North
—	1◇
2♠	4♠
6♠	No

Not that many modern players would force with two spades or jump from two spades to four spades. Such sensible bids would not occur to them.

West leads the queen of hearts and South wins. The hand is a fairly simple exercise in suit establishment; South needs to establish a long trick in diamonds and must be careful to preserve entries to the dummy.

It would be a bad mistake to draw more than just one round of trumps—with the queen, of course. This is the full hand:

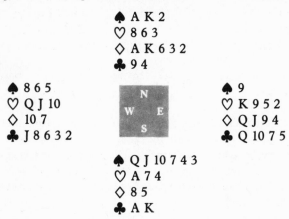

                    ♠ A K 2
                    ♡ 8 6 3
                    ◇ A K 6 3 2
                    ♣ 9 4

    ♠ 8 6 5   ♠ 9
    ♡ Q J 10   ♡ K 9 5 2
    ◇ 10 7   ◇ Q J 9 4
    ♣ J 8 6 3 2   ♣ Q 10 7 5

                    ♠ Q J 10 7 4 3
                    ♡ A 7 4
                    ◇ 8 5
                    ♣ A K

Having won the heart lead, you cash the queen of spades, then play three rounds of diamonds, ruffing high. Then play a spade to the king, ruff the next diamond with a high trump, and after drawing the last spade you have twelve tricks. You began with eleven winners and the long diamond is the twelfth.

14.   ♠ A 7 4
                ♡ Q 3 2
                ◇ A Q 10 8 5 2
                ♣ Q

♠ Q led

                ♠ K 6
                ♡ A 10 8 5
                ◇ K
                ♣ A 8 6 5 3 2

The bidding goes:

South	North
—	1◇
2♣	2◇
2♡	2♠
3NT	No

North's two spades in this sequence is the fourth suit and not necessarily a biddable suit. North is saying "If you have a guard in spades as well, then bid notrumps." South, evidently, is strong enough to jump to game. West leads the queen of spades. How do you plan the play?

Answer: This is another exercise in overcoming a blocked position. You may think it natural to win with the king of spades, cash the king of diamonds, and lead a low heart. Even if the queen loses to the king you still have a spade entry to the table and will have no problem if diamonds are 3–3 or if the jack is doubleton. None of these good things happen when the distribution is:

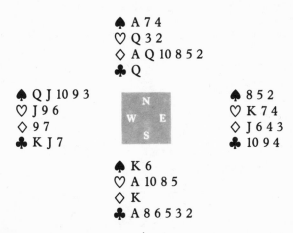

```
              ♠ A 7 4
              ♡ Q 3 2
              ◇ A Q 10 8 5 2
              ♣ Q

♠ Q J 10 9 3          N          ♠ 8 5 2
♡ J 9 6          W         E     ♡ K 7 4
◇ 9 7                 S          ◇ J 6 4 3
♣ K J 7                          ♣ 10 9 4

              ♠ K 6
              ♡ A 10 8 5
              ◇ K
              ♣ A 8 6 5 3 2
```

If you played in the fashion described above—king of diamonds, then a low heart to the queen and king—you failed to take into account that you needed only five diamond tricks for game and could give yourself an extra chance by overtaking the king of diamonds with the ace and following with the queen. If diamonds are 3–3 you have nine tricks—and there is the additional chance that there may be doubleton 9 x. When the nine falls on the second round you clear the suit and make game with two spades, one heart, five diamonds and one club.

15.
     ♠ 10 7 3
     ♡ J 7 3 2
     ◊ 10 8 2
     ♣ A Q 10

♡K led

     ♠ A K Q 8 4 2
     ♡ —
     ◊ K J 9 4
     ♣ 6 4 2

You play in four spades and West begins with the king of hearts. You ruff and draw two rounds of trumps, to which all follow. How do you continue?

Answer: Suppose you begin with a finesse of the ten of clubs, losing to the jack. East leads a diamond and you will go down if the hand is like this:

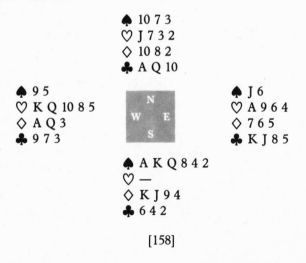

     ♠ 10 7 3
     ♡ J 7 3 2
     ◊ 10 8 2
     ♣ A Q 10

♠ 9 5   ♠ J 6
♡ K Q 10 8 5   ♡ A 9 6 4
◊ A Q 3   ◊ 7 6 5
♣ 9 7 3   ♣ K J 8 5

     ♠ A K Q 8 4 2
     ♡ —
     ◊ K J 9 4
     ♣ 6 4 2

After the trumps have broken 2–2, the contract is cast-iron. Just lead a diamond from hand at trick four. As the cards lie, West may win and lead a club to the queen and king. East returns a diamond, but now you will be able to discard a club from dummy on the fourth round of diamonds.

Suppose, alternatively, that the low diamond at trick four were to lose to the queen in East's hand. There would still be nothing the defence could do to prevent you from establishing a discard on the fourth diamond. You should see that if you play on diamonds first you will surely make ten tricks with six spades, two diamonds, one club and one ruff.

16.
         ♠ A 10 9 4
         ♡ K 9 2
         ◇ 3
         ♣ A K J 3 2

◇ Q led

         ♠ K 8 7
         ♡ A 8 3
         ◇ K 10 8 2
         ♣ 10 5 4

North opens one club, East passes, and since 1NT over one club normally signifies about 8 to 10 points, South responds 1NT. North has just enough to bid two spades and now South goes to 3NT.

West leads the queen of diamonds, which is allowed to hold. He follows with a low diamond, won by the eight. How should South play now?

Answer: It is fairly clear that West is the danger hand. So, instead of taking the club finesse, which is the percentage play with eight cards, you should play off ace and king. The point is that you can afford to lose a club to West, but not to East, when the cards lie like this:

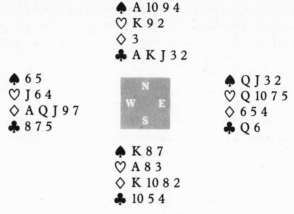

```
                    ♠ A 10 9 4
                    ♡ K 9 2
                    ◇ 3
                    ♣ A K J 3 2
♠ 6 5                              ♠ Q J 3 2
♡ J 6 4            N               ♡ Q 10 7 5
◇ A Q J 9 7     W     E            ◇ 6 5 4
♣ 8 7 5            S               ♣ Q 6
                    ♠ K 8 7
                    ♡ A 8 3
                    ◇ K 10 8 2
                    ♣ 10 5 4
```

After playing off the top clubs you will make at least ten tricks. Note that the same type of play would be correct if the clubs were something like A Q J x x opposite 10 9 x. You would play the ace first because you could afford to lose a trick to the left-hand opponent.

17.   ♠ A Q 2
              ♡ A 3
              ◇ 6 4 3
              ♣ A K 7 4 2

♠8 led

              ♠ 9 6 3
              ♡ K Q J 10 8 2
              ◇ A K
              ♣ 6 5

North opens one club and South, just short of the high-card strength needed for a jump, responds one heart. North has an awkward call now; he might bid 2NT, despite the weakness in diamonds, but most players would rebid one spade. South jumps to four hearts (3NT would not be a mistake) and North goes to six hearts.

West leads the eight of spades. How would you play in six hearts?

Answer: This contract may depend on what you do on the first trick. It is quite possible that West, leading through the hand that has bid spades, may hold the king, but to insert the queen might be a bad mistake. Suppose that the cards lie like this:

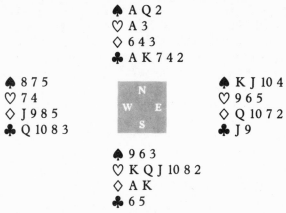

```
                    ♠ A Q 2
                    ♡ A 3
                    ◇ 6 4 3
                    ♣ A K 7 4 2

  ♠ 8 7 5                          ♠ K J 10 4
  ♡ 7 4              N             ♡ 9 6 5
  ◇ J 9 8 5       W     E          ◇ Q 10 7 2
  ♣ Q 10 8 3         S             ♣ J 9

                    ♠ 9 6 3
                    ♡ K Q J 10 8 2
                    ◇ A K
                    ♣ 6 5
```

If you insert the queen of spades on the opening lead, East will win and return the jack. You will be obliged to win with the ace and thereafter will be short of entries to make a trick with dummy's fifth club.

It is essential to play a low spade from dummy on the opening lead. East will win and return a diamond. Now you play three rounds of clubs, followed by king of hearts and a heart to the ace. Then you ruff another club, draw the outstanding trump, and still have a spade entry to dummy. Your third spade will go away on dummy's fifth club.

18.
```
                    ♠ Q J 2
                    ♡ A 3 2
                    ◇ K J 8 2
                    ♣ 7 6 4
```

♡K led

```
                    ♠ K 6 4 3
                    ♡ 6 5 4
                    ◇ A Q 6 3
                    ♣ A J
```

Playing a 12–14 notrump, South opens 1NT, North raises to 2NT and South bids the game. West leads the king of hearts. How should South plan the play?

Answer: To begin with, it is probably right to win the heart lead, hoping that the suit will break 4–3. If you hold off for a round or two the opponents may switch to clubs.

Having won the heart lead you play the king of diamonds, followed by the *eight* of diamonds to the queen. Why the eight? You will see in a moment.

You lead a low spade to the queen, which holds. Don't follow with the jack of spades, because West may now hold the ace alone and you need three spade tricks to make this borderline contract. Observe the full hand:

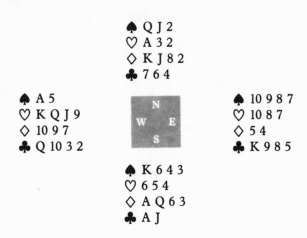

```
                    ♠ Q J 2
                    ♡ A 3 2
                    ◇ K J 8 2
                    ♣ 7 6 4

    ♠ A 5              N          ♠ 10 9 8 7
    ♡ K Q J 9       W   E        ♡ 10 8 7
    ◇ 10 9 7           S          ◇ 5 4
    ♣ Q 10 3 2                    ♣ K 9 8 5

                    ♠ K 6 4 3
                    ♡ 6 5 4
                    ◇ A Q 6 3
                    ♣ A J
```

After the queen of spades return to hand with the jack of diamonds to the ace and lead another spade. After West has made the ace of spades and cashed three heart winners, the position will be:

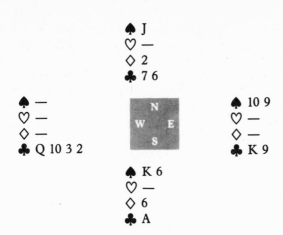

```
              ♠ J
              ♡ —
              ◇ 2
              ♣ 7 6
♠ —                        ♠ 10 9
♡ —          N            ♡ —
◇ —       W     E         ◇ —
♣ Q 10 3 2    S            ♣ K 9
              ♠ K 6
              ♡ —
              ◇ 6
              ♣ A
```

When you win with the ace of clubs you lead a low spade to the jack and return to the six of diamonds to make the last spade. Go through the hand again. You will find that all these precautions were necessary.

19.
     ♠ A J 5
     ♡ A J 10 9 8
     ◇ 10 3
     ♣ K 3 2

♣ J led
     ♠ K 10 6
     ♡ K Q
     ◇ A Q 9 2
     ♣ A Q 6 4

Many players would open 2NT on the South hand, but this is a slight exaggeration, with five points wrapped up in the doubleton K Q of hearts. Also, the hand contains three queens, and queens are slightly overvalued in the 4–3–2–1 count. So, we prefer one diamond. The bidding may then go like this:

South	North
1◇	1♡
3NT	6NT
No	

West leads the jack of clubs and East plays low. How do you plan the play?

Answer: There are eleven tricks on top and numerous chances for a twelfth: a 3–3 break in clubs, a double finesse in diamonds, a finesse in spades. It would not be *too* bad to win with the queen of clubs, cross to dummy on the second round of hearts, then run the ten of diamonds. If this loses to the jack you will still have several chances—you can play for the break in clubs, for the queen of spades to fall in two rounds, and finally you may need to take a second finesse in diamonds.

The contract is certainly odds on if you play this way, but you might fail if the cards lay like this:

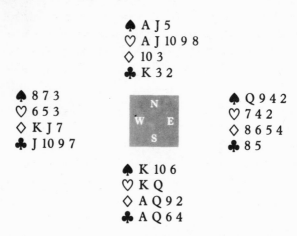

```
            ♠ A J 5
            ♡ A J 10 9 8
            ◇ 10 3
            ♣ K 3 2

♠ 8 7 3                      ♠ Q 9 4 2
♡ 6 5 3          N           ♡ 7 4 2
◇ K J 7      W       E       ◇ 8 6 5 4
♣ J 10 9 7       S           ♣ 8 5

            ♠ K 10 6
            ♡ K Q
            ◇ A Q 9 2
            ♣ A Q 6 4
```

If you lose this contract, don't blame your luck. After winning the club lead play three rounds of hearts, then test the clubs. When you find that West holds the long club, simply let him win the fourth club, and then any return will give you your twelfth trick. Note one point: it would be a mistake to play off even one more round of hearts before the throw-in, because the discard from your own hand would be awkward.

20.

♠ A 8 7 4 2
♡ 6 3
◇ Q 6 5
♣ A K 8

♣Q led

♠ K Q J 10 6 3
♡ A Q
◇ J 9 4
♣ 6 4

Playing in four spades, you win the opening club lead and draw the trumps in one round. It would be disappointing to go down in this contract, especially as your side wasn't far from advancing towards a slam. Can you make a certainty of the game?

Answer: Suppose that everything lies badly, as in this diagram:

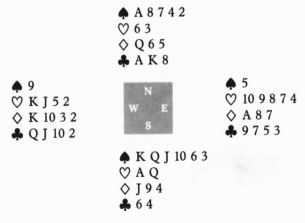

♠ A 8 7 4 2
♡ 6 3
◇ Q 6 5
♣ A K 8

♠ 9
♡ K J 5 2
◇ K 10 3 2
♣ Q J 10 2

♠ 5
♡ 10 9 8 7 4
◇ A 8 7
♣ 9 7 5 3

♠ K Q J 10 6 3
♡ A Q
◇ J 9 4
♣ 6 4

Was it your intention to win the club lead, draw trumps, and begin with a finesse of the queen of hearts? West will win and exit with a second club. In the end you will have to try a finesse of the nine of diamonds and you will find you are one down.

If you remembered the section on elimination play in an earlier chapter, you will have made this contract. Simply eliminate the clubs, then play ace and queen of hearts. Now the opponents will be forced either to concede a ruff-and-discard or to open up the diamonds.

Well, how many of these twenty questions did you get right—or nearly right? About half? That's good. You're on your way!

Index